CW01500563

Reading My Mother Back

Reading My Mother Back

A Memoir in Childhood Animal Stories

Timothy C. Baker

Goldsmiths
Press

Copyright © 2022 Goldsmiths Press
First published in 2022 by Goldsmiths Press
Goldsmiths, University of London, New Cross
London SE14 6NW

Printed and bound by Versa Press, USA
Distribution by the MIT Press
Cambridge, Massachusetts, and London, England

Copyright © 2022 Timothy C. Baker

A CIP record for this book is available from the British Library

ISBN 978-1-913380-47-2 (hbk)
ISBN 978-1-913380-46-5 (ebk)

www.gold.ac.uk/goldsmiths-press

Goldsmiths
UNIVERSITY OF LONDON

To Fitree

The Story of Babar

Funerals are easy. There are surprises, of course – the weight of the coffin and the terrible fear it might slip as you walk down the aisle, the need to memorise attendance, the fact that you don't cry – but so much of the day is occupied with pleasantries, with small talk, with setting up and packing up the food at the reception, that you can distract yourself. 'Thank you.' 'Me too.' 'I'm just here until Monday.' 'Thank you.' The same conversations again and again, a lulling rhythm of condolence.

The day after the funeral is hard. You wake up in your childhood home, in a guest bed overladen with wool blankets, although you can't get warm. And you're alone. Your father is out, somewhere, with someone. You eat some pasta salad left over from the reception. You watch half of a ball game, not caring who's playing. You pace, and you pace, and you pace. And then you search.

For years you've been so sure your mother was working on a secret project. She loved words, she loved pens and blank books, she loved stories. And her story was so extraordinary, so singular, she must have wanted to preserve it. So you start simply, in her desk. A few plans for garden designs, drawn so carefully there was never a chance of them being realised. A few calligraphic exercises. Some blank cards, just in case. But nothing. You start to panic. You look in the leaves of books she loved, under the bed, in wastebaskets, in the violin case and through the sheet music that is still laid out, in every corner of the house. You spend hours wondering what you're missing. But there is nothing. Your mother has died, and there are no words. She has already begun to disappear.

So this is the story of my mother, and of her death. And I cannot tell you her story, not really, and so I must rely on the stories of others. Much of what follows is apocryphal. Almost certainly some of it is misremembered. But there is no one left who knows the whole truth, and the stories are what I have. So this is the story of a woman who told her own stories, and told others; it is the story I have to tell to make her real. And it is the story, just as much, of the stories we shared, and of the animals that filled them, a world of fable and romance that we lived in, talked about, ran away from, abided by. For my mother was a reader, and I am a reader. And all I can do now is read back to her.

Marie Helen Lefler was born on 23 September 1955 to two teachers, their oldest child. Their names might not be important here. Her birth certificate shows that she was born in Washington, DC. Her parents did not live in Washington, and there were plenty of available hospitals in their Baltimore neighbourhood. Someone, for some reason, decided she shouldn't be registered there. Or maybe there was a problem, never revealed, never spoken of. But she was born in the wrong city, the first displacement, the first secret, of all the rest.

The stories of her childhood don't cohere. Much of it was spent in Baltimore, in a series of lower-middle-class and immigrant neighbourhoods, some of it in New Jersey, where she stayed only long enough to pick up some Yiddish that would pop up unexpectedly in conversation later in her life. At some point, when she was in middle school, the family seems to have fled New Jersey, perhaps because her father struck someone with his car. Once my mother speculated that her father had killed a boy in a hit-and-run, a story my father cautiously confirms; certainly my grandfather had a breakdown of some sort. He taught algebra, which neither my mother nor I could ever master. I cannot recall what he looked like, but remember vividly a description of him standing over the stove, cooking pasta, the sauce running down his bare chest, through what my mother described as surprisingly pendulous breasts. He worked as a bellhop, too, proud to have carried the bags of Stevie Wonder the first time he came to Baltimore. Her mother might have worked, might not have; she became a teacher and a Catholic later in life, I believe, although I do not know if either conversion was a surprise. There was a sister, born a few years after my mother. Her stories are not the same ones. The four of them lived in Baltimore, and they hated each other, and my mother looked for escape. And her escape was a farm.

Her mother's parents were, by her account, kind people. Their farm was not a farm, simply a suburban outpost, but there is a picture, now lost, of her standing next to them, wheat or cornfields in the background, so perhaps it was a farm after all. My great-grandfather was a chemist who, my mother said, invented a formula for artificial orange flavouring that was used for many years. I am named after him, by virtue of an agricultural pun. My mother's grandmother was, well, I don't know. She was a Mohawk Indian, my mother said, or she was from the West Indies, and her surname, Jones, came from a Welsh sailor who was stationed there. Both stories existed, neither is necessarily true. She learned to cook in Louisiana. She never became a citizen. She was, I've heard, a servant for a family during the Spanish flu epidemic, and tended to the dying. I do not know who her family was, or where they lived, or where they died. I do not know why she left Louisiana. I do not know her people, her ethnicity, her sorrows. I do not know who she was, except that she loved my mother, and her recipe for biscuits is the best I've ever found. Her cookbook, handwritten, is also named with a pun. The biscuit recipe is on page eleven, and whatever the recipe was originally titled, they were only called 'Page 11 Biscuits'.

These are not shoring fragments; they do not form a picture. There are gaps, lies, misrememberings. My mother did not claim any childhood friends, although surely there must have been some. She did not speak about her school, about her neighbourhood, about her home. She spoke about a legacy of violence, and didn't speak of it. Her world, from childhood, was already asunder, never to be repaired, never to be whole.

So I have to start with a different story, *The Story of Babar*. In 1983–84, Jean and Laurent de Brunhoff were given a touring exhibition of watercolours, celebrating *Fifty Years of Babar*. It visited Minneapolis, Washington, DC, San Diego, San Jose, Evanston, Cedar Rapids, and Baltimore, and consisted of 214 drawings of Babar, 87 by Jean and 127 by Laurent. I like these numbers, this itinerary, the fact that I can sit in my office in a university in northern Scotland and find something that seems reassuringly true. My parents and I saw the exhibition in Baltimore, of course.

Picture us. I am five years old, and the pictures are mounted slightly too high for me. I crane my head up, and behind the waists and forearms of the adults around me I can see the elephants at play. It is my first time in a museum, and I am grateful there are elephants there.

But I am slightly scared as well, because Babar has long been my most vivid nightmare. You might know the story already – you must. Babar appears as an infant, in a hammock, his mother rocking him to sleep. It is an intimate image, dominated by the green of the trees and the grey of the elephants, with birds, butterflies, and flowers all appearing in the same red accent. It does not prepare you for the two-page spread that follows, thirty-one elephants (and two monkeys) at play, against vivid pink hills. There is no end to the elephants' activities. They chase each other and swim, they build forts in the sand, they play catch and, more curiously, rugby. They are very happy elephants.

And then disaster strikes. Two parallel images, on facing pages: Babar is riding on his mother's back, content, while a hunter fires and a monkey and two birds look on; Babar weeps over his mother's corpse, while the hunter scurries to steal him away and the other animals flee. The mother is dead, the world is asunder, the pastoral of the opening pages cannot be restored. And this is not what scares me. What scares me doesn't arrive until page thirty-four. Again, two parallel images, this time to be read vertically. The King of the elephants stands alone, holding a mushroom to his mouth; the King of the elephants falls down, green and wobbly, his crown askew, his skin beginning to sag.

I do not know for how many years I was haunted by a poisoned King of the elephants in my sleep, but enough that the image still gives me shivers. Babar's mother dies instantly; she is there and then not there. But the King of the elephants suffers, and that suffering is palpable and heart-rending. I tell this story to my students, I show them the pictures, and they laugh at me, and I can still hardly bear the horror of what I'm seeing.

And standing in the Baltimore Museum of Art, I see the saggy King in front of me, glorious and green and in pain. And this is the first lesson. Because in this setting, it is not a scary image, but beautiful, in its way. I am with my parents, and this death is something I can take in, and walk away from. It does not transfigure me. The suffering I find in a book is not the suffering I find in art; the private hurts me more, leaves a deeper mark.

The Story of Babar is a strange book, really. It is a story of maturation, of growth in the world, of a move from apparently primitive to apparently more civilised states. Its colonial overtones are difficult to ignore, and slightly sour in the mouth. Babar learns how to be human – where human seems to be defined as French, white, and wealthy – how to read and do addition, how to drive and use a lift and wear a bright green suit, greener than the trees or the dying king. Babar and Celeste wear beautiful clothes, unlike the other elephants. He brings harmony to his people, like a good king, and yet is always removed from them. It is unclear whom the child reader should want to emulate. Babar is like them, lives a familiar life; the other elephants seem to be having a lot more fun, most of the time. Who would not want to be one of the elephants playing beneath the trees? Who would want to be civilised?

Because this is the secret of Babar. We read it for a story of growth, of maturation, of how possible it is, how easy, to leave your world and return better, more sophisticated, more knowing. All you need, it seems, is for your mother to die, and a spot of light kidnapping. But we want to be one of the unnamed elephants, dancing and swimming and in love with the world as it is. We want a story of joyful stasis, and the book can't provide it. The world can't provide it. We are ripped, by education, by death, from the world we most desire.

And this is my mother's story, of course. No king of the elephants she, nor queen, and no finery or fancy motorcars. But the need to tell a story of how you left the world, how you moved past violence, how you became yourself by being someone else. I cannot tell you about my mother's childhood. If anyone can, I do not know them, I have not met them. But I can tell you that her story has to be false, to make it true, and that the very worst things in it are the ones that are real. My mother did not leave her own story behind, but picture her there, just for a minute, standing in a museum in a city she sometimes hated and kept returning to, holding her son's hand, watching the King of the elephants die. Imagine that she is beautiful. Imagine she can tell you a story. Imagine that it's true.

Merle the High Flying Squirrel

It is mid-November 1984, and I am upstairs in my bedroom, in a small house in Catonsville, Maryland, reading. It is a school day, and I am ecstatic not to be at school. I'm supposed to be the sort of child who loves school. I certainly look the part, with my pudgy features and my bowl cut and the stack of books under my arm. But I am in suburban Baltimore, in a community where everyone works for the government, and there's just been an election. And the news of Ronald Reagan's victory has been announced, and I have cried in front of everyone in my class, to the laughter and scorn of my first-grade teacher. And so I am off school, sick, or sick enough, and I am reading, and I am safe.

I have been reading for less than a year, and for all my life. My mother, in her apparent wisdom, banned me from books until I was four, on the suspicion she would never get to speak to me again. And yet in the surviving pictures from that time, there are always books there, carried behind me in a little red wagon, my own assurance of a future world. And once I started, I couldn't stop. In 1984 and 1985 I read every picture-book in my classroom library, and every chapter-book too, at the same time. I read every Hardy Boys and Nancy Drew. I read the books for girls who liked horses and boys who liked sports, without particularly liking either horses or sports or, indeed, other children. I got permission to use the big kids' library so I could write book reports on the great trifecta of my childhood: Lewis, L'Engle, and Tolkien. I don't know a story of development that lets me go, in the span of a year, from not reading at all to reading *The Hobbit* every three months, but once there were books, there was nothing else.

But of course there was so much else. There was a whole world. And the world was terrifying. The same teacher who mocked my Mondale support gave us nuclear drills, the kind you see in 1950s educational films, where children hide underneath their desks. My education took place not just in the Cold War, but in an earlier version of that never-ending war than the one I actually inhabited. Every account I can find, every history book, says that these drills ended in the early 1960s, and yet I vividly remember the metal legs of the desks as we crouched beneath. I remember the terror and the tedium. I remember, even then, the absurdity of the entire enterprise. I remember wondering, even a year or two later, if these memories were real.

My political education began earlier. My first memory is of New Year's 1980, and I am at a leftist, Christian, anti-war party, and keep dancing long after the adults are pooped. As I was 367 days old at that moment, this cannot be my memory, and yet there it is, the feel of the floor under my butt, the rhythm of the music. The first time I get my picture in the newspaper is five years later, when I am at a protest outside the Pentagon, and we have wrapped the building in a giant quilt. My mother's panel depicts my family in a canoe, on a lake in Vermont. I am pictured sitting on the building's steps, with my ragged bowl haircut and flannel shirt, because the Harrison Ford film *Witness* has just come out and I look enough like Lukas Haas in that film to be newsworthy. Later, when we move to Vermont, my father will buy all of his clothes from an Amish supply company. There were always protests, there was always anger, there were always communities of resistance.

But on this day in November I'm reading Bill Peet's *Merle the High Flying Squirrel*. It might not be a book you know, if you did not grow up in the United States, or if you weren't a child in the late 1970s and early 1980s. Peet worked for Disney for many years, and was behind my favourite animated films of theirs, *101 Dalmatians* and *The Sword in the Stone*, although I did not know this at the time, since my only access to Disney was a beautiful gold-covered hardback that told the stories of each of their features in a handful of pages, a book I borrowed again and again from the library without ever having seen the films. But his illustrations in *Merle*, and his other picture-books, are softer; you can see the lines, almost the imprint, of the coloured pencils.

Merle is not a happy squirrel at the book's start. He is, indeed, a 'timid frightened little squirrel' who lives nervously in a city park, scared of both the people and the buildings around him. Yet, as the story begins, he decides that he is tired of being scared all the time; he eavesdrops on a group of men, one of whom tells stories about the beauty of the tall trees out West, and this story is so exciting that Merle decides that he must see these trees for himself. He first sets out along telephone wires. At the city limits he finds a kite, decorated with a crude smiley face, that has become tangled in the wires; as he attempts to free its tail, for the benefit of the children below, he gets swept away, first in a storm, then a tornado, until, at last, he lands on a giant redwood. Merle is finally happy; the trees make him feel small, but their beauty is sufficient.

Reading Peet's book now is a strange experience. Like many books read in childhood, it is much shorter than I remember; it begins and ends quite abruptly, so that the reader learns very little about Merle's life outside this one adventure. Although positioned as a story about the benefits of risk-taking and bravery, the events are largely accidental and unlikely, as Merle seems to cross the continental United States in the space of a day. It is a story of escape, to be sure, but it is specifically an escape to quietness; although a bird is pictured on the final page, Merle does not speak to anyone but himself, or hear anyone but himself, throughout the second half of the book. And this is perplexing, because one of the first things the reader learns about Merle is that he loves, above all else, listening to other people's stories. Stories are what allow him to imagine another life, but once he achieves that life, there is no need for stories any more, and there the picture-book ends.

It is, in some ways, a melancholy book, a story of wilful seclusion and isolation. It is the perfect book to give a child who cannot understand the world around him, perhaps, a child who cannot speak to people with any ease, but who already wants something beautiful, something true. And there it is, on the second page. Merle is sitting in a tree, listening to the conversations of the old men beneath him, and the tree is scored with the names of passersby, carved into the bark, and at the centre of the names is my own, a 'Tim' surrounded by Kathy, Ramona, and the cryptic initials J.O.H.

It is something of a truism in the academic study of children's literature that stories of anthropomorphised animals are used to increase children's empathy. Somewhere between half and three-quarters of picture-books feature anthropomorphised animal characters. Gail F. Melson, in *Why the Wild Things Are: Animals in the Lives of Children*, argues that 'animal characters are the raw material out of which children construct a sense of self', while Tess Cosslett, in *Talking Animals in British Children's Fiction, 1786-1914*, claims that links between human and animal consciousness can be used 'to give moral lessons on child behaviour'. Already we have two fundamental directions of travel: either children naturally empathise with nonhuman animals because both the animals and children must navigate an adult world that is foreign, filled with strange rules and customs, or adults find animal stories a more efficient means of instilling moral values in children. And children's animal stories can change the world: perhaps the first, and most significant, such book, Anna Sewell's

Black Beauty, which you might remember is presented as the autobiography of the titular horse, was instrumental in the move towards anti-cruelty legislation in both the United States and the United Kingdom. Either way, however, our childhood reading is filled with animals. Animals might not teach us empathy, but it is with animals that we first empathise; they share our grief and joy, they form the literary community into which we are first immersed.

And it is a strange, and strangely consistent, animal world. Nonhuman animals share a language with each other, but not with humans, although usually they can understand human speech. It is rare that a goose and a cat cannot easily converse, but rarer still that a child might enter into that dialogue. The animal community is one of all those left outside the human world, automatically bonded together. In most farmyard stories the reader will find only one or two representatives of any given species; all nonhuman creatures are subsumed under the singular category of 'animal'. The human world itself is full of threat: farm animals believe they will be eaten, wild animals believe they will be hunted, pets and companion animals simply seem to have a disturbingly high mortality rate. Reading *Charlotte's Web*, or *Bambi*, or *Old Yeller*, or *Where the Red Fern Grows* is how we learn that the world is cruel, mysterious, and unforgiving; it is where we often learn that adults are not to be trusted. As in Peet's story, the moral lesson, if there is one, is about the value of separation rather than incorporation. Animal stories teach us, with surprising frequency, about death and loss. They tell us that the world is fragile, that the company of others, or at least human others, is unsustainable. What we remember, most of all, about the animal stories we read as children is that animals die. If there is a dog, it will die, and the child protagonist will mourn, and the child reader will mourn, and they will learn something of their own mortality. Almost as often, however, there is a story where it is the human who dies, usually a parent, and a dog appears as what the critic Michelle Superle calls a 'transforming substance', a catalyst who helps, again, the child protagonist come to terms with their loss and learn, essentially, to love again. The child reader sees animals as both self and other, as separated from the world and the best the world has to offer, as what must be lost and what is still loved.

More recently scholars have carried out empirical studies that suggest these claims of empathy and morality may have been overstated. Nicole E. Larsen, Kang Lee, and Patricia A. Ganea, writing in *Developmental Science* in 2018, conclude that while 'children clearly enjoy immersing themselves in hypothetical worlds', 'fantastical stories may not be as effective for teaching real-world knowledge or real-life social behaviors as realistic ones'. Children might, they say, learn to share more readily, or be kinder to each other, when they see children doing these things in books, rather than nonhuman animals. Children may not confuse themselves with animals as often as the scholarship suggests. Children might just dismiss fanciful animal stories as not relevant to their experience.

But children, of course, already live in a fantastical world, a world in which everything connects, in which everything contributes to a single story. The tornado that takes Merle to California is no different to the tornado that takes Dorothy to Oz, which is no different to the tornado that destroys my parents' few possessions when they live, on the cusp of twenty, on a farm in Missouri, and from which they flee. And they bring with them a few surviving books, notably boxed editions of *The Chronicles of Narnia* and *The Lord of the Rings*, still water-damaged, much loved. And lying in my bed in 1984, reading *Merle*, I can look at the cracks in the ceiling above my bed, and be confident that they form a map of

Narnia. Our understanding of the world, as children, is entirely hypothetical: we look for moments we can cling to, which seem to explain the world around us, and if they are voiced by talking animals, so much the better. And animals, of course, are often ornery and unpleasant, and this is often their attraction: I loved Frog and Toad, that model of dysfunctional relationships, because the characters were selfish and sad.

And animals teach us how to tell stories. Level 2 of the I Can Read series, which published many of my favourite stories, including the Frog and Toad tales, is designated 'Reading with Help', and many of the volumes are collections of short stories, usually with a cumulative effect. Else Holmelund Minarik's *Little Bear's Friend*, with illustrations by Maurice Sendak, contains four linked stories, with their own titles. The first, 'Little Bear and Emily', opens with Little Bear sitting alone in a tree, much like Merle, looking at the world spread out before him. He looks at the town, the mountains, and the sea, and he feels the wind in his fur. He is visited by squirrels and birds and a worm who ask him to play, but he declines, for he must go home for lunch. On his way he meets a little girl, Emily, and her dolly Lucy, and they walk together and share cookies; when he gets home, he tells his mother everything that has just happened to him. His story celebrates his new friendship with Emily, but even more the power of storytelling; it is only as he recounts his adventures that the extent of his new friendship is revealed. In the second story Little Bear, Lucy, and Emily meet a duck, who is added to their friendship group; in the third the four of them go to a party with an owl; in the final story, Little Bear writes a letter to Emily telling her of all other animals. Stories grow as they are shared. Each story adds new characters, but also adds new layers of storytelling, so that the second telling is as important as the first. The book ends with Little Bear alone again, sending Emily love from Owl, Duck, Hen, and Cat, and looking forward to the summer when they can all play together again. Writing the story makes it real; the page becomes the place where each of these different characters, one from each species, can fully coexist.

In Arnold Lobel's *Mouse Soup* and *Mouse Tales*, similarly, stories are shown to have real power in the world, whether in helping a mouse father send his children to sleep or, more excitingly, fighting off hungry weasels. The stories animals tell are connected, and they matter in the world: they have a capacity to change. In Lobel's and Minarik's works the animal protagonists are clearly anthropomorphised: they wear human clothes, eat meals at appropriate times off suitable tableware, and go promptly to bed. The stories themselves, though, are sometimes clearly fantastical – a tired mouse passes a person selling feet, and buys himself new ones – and sometimes simply fantastical in an everyday way, where there are no conflicts between predator and prey, but only a harmonious community. What matters is simply that the world is known through stories. In 'Dragons and Giants', from Lobel's *Frog and Toad Together*, Frog and Toad read a book of fairy tales, and wonder if they are as brave as the protagonists. They try to have adventures: they climb a mountain, they are threatened by a snake and a hawk, and they finally flee to their home, where Toad cowers in bed with his covers pulled over his head, and Frog hides in the cupboard. They feel, says Lobel, 'very brave together'. It is our stories, not our actions, that show us our place in the world.

And my childhood world was full of animals and stories; indeed, there were always animals around, more than people. The house on Kingston Road in Catonsville where we lived in 1984 and 1985 looks quite peculiar when I pull it up on Google Street View now: a front that combines brick and stonework, stucco, and faux-Tudor wooden beams to no good effect. Just in the corner, though, you can see a dilapidated garage, which when we lived there was home to forty or so rabbits, mainly kept for meat or sale. Every Easter we ate a sacrificial Easter Bunny. I'm told this explains things about me. The driveway was tilled, and filled with tomato plants and other vegetables. I do not remember other children, although I am sure there must have been some, but I remember the rabbits. Across the street was a funeral home with a great green expanse of lawn, where I first outran my mother in a short race, but our yard remained magical, filled with flowers and vegetables and life.

And it is in this house that my first great memory of reading was formed. It's a small memory, one that could have been made any day, but happened sometime in the summer of 1985. I am sitting in the living room, in an old William Morris-style armchair, reading one of the later Oz books. It's odd that I remember Oz so well since Baum, like Lewis Carroll, always made me feel slightly nauseated; the worlds of those fictions did not cohere enough, were too absurd for comfort. My mother is in the kitchen, making a loaf of bread, part of a brief period where she determined to live up to the Baker name, perhaps, and made bread not only for the family, but also for communion at a local church. And when the loaf is finished, she slices off the heel, and butters it, and brings it to me.

It is a memory that belongs in a picture-book. The scene could come straight from Minarik's Little Bear series, with their Maurice Sendak illustrations and their focus on a doting mother always at home, ready to listen to her son's stories, and echoes the final line – 'and it was still hot' – of Sendak's *Where the Wild Things Are*. It is a scene of domestic harmony that seems so conflict-free, so idealised, it is hard to believe in. And yet there it is: I am alone, I am reading, my mother is there, I have a slice of bread, and the world is whole.

I do not know if I knew my mother was sick at that point. I suspect I didn't, or if I did, it seemed part of the natural order of things. That my mother did not work was not unusual in the religious community we were a part of, where women's employment – indeed, any signs of women's independent thought – was generally frowned upon. That my mother did not have many close friends might seem more strange, but then, neither did I, or not the sort of friends who would visit my house. There were books, there were rabbits, there was my mother, and the outer world might not have existed.

The French phenomenologist Gaston Bachelard describes this condition well. No world, he says, will ever be as real to us, as richly imagined, as our childhood home. Our memories are most real to us when they are fixed in space; he opens his study of houses with the claim that 'imagination augments the values of reality'. The childhood home is a poetic world, a world of memory and imagination that defines us as we define it. This scene of reading is a scene I have made real by remembering, by imagining, by believing it to have explanatory potential, by fervently hoping that it might say something about my life. And this, for someone like Bachelard, is right, and natural, and perhaps inevitable. The stories we tell about our houses are not simply descriptive, but formative.

I knew, of course, that my mother was scared of the outside world, as nervous as Merle in his tree, listening to other people's stories but never being a part of them. I knew this because she drove me to school. My mother learned to drive at twenty-nine, specifically in order to take me to school, a distance of less than two miles, but which necessitated crossing the Baltimore Beltway. For two years she drove those four miles every day, terrified, and when we moved from Baltimore she never drove again. She was not scared of cars as such; indeed, later in life, when she was far less mobile and we were living in rural Vermont, her idea of fun was to have my father drive her to a nearby city, Northampton or Amherst, Massachusetts, and to park on the side of the road, and simply sit there for hours, watching people walk by. She would never speak to anyone, rarely unrolled the windows, but being in a car, watching the world, was still a form of freedom. It was the control, the responsibility, of driving that she refused.

I inherited that fear. I failed my license test three times when I was sixteen, and have never tried again. Even being a passenger scares me. I sit tight. I lock the door, out of fear I might suddenly jump. It's hard to open my eyes. And in the fantastical world of youth, where everything is connected, it was somehow inevitably after one of those failed tests, sitting in a Chinese diner in Springfield, Vermont, that my mother told me she would die, that she had always been going to die, that it might come any day, although it would not come for nine more years.

Not driving, for my mother, was more than dislike, or fear. It was a recognition that stasis was her best form of escape. That staying put, knowing one space, imagining that space fully, was a form of survival. It's why she spent so much time drawing intricate plans of houses she would never live in, gardens she would never have the strength to manage. It was vital to imagine herself in a space she could control, the space she had been denied throughout her childhood, perhaps throughout her adulthood too, and for her, for me, that imagination was, sometimes, enough.

The school I was attending had, itself, a slightly dubious history. In its former incarnation as St Timothy's Hall, it had been an Episcopalian military academy known for its rigorous discipline; its most notorious student was John Wilkes Booth. When I was a student there the discipline had inevitably lapsed, and I remember no military connections, but there was still a plaque to Booth hanging on the wall, whether in praise or censure I do not know. And yet it was a world in which Reagan was king, a world of uniforms and equal time devoted to love of God and love of country. And it was a school out of time. The map of the solar system on the wall of my first-grade classroom predated Pluto's classification as a planet. The lesson plans seemed of similar vintage, although I still remember the song that taught us long vowels, and would sing it for you now.

Just as I do not know where my mother's childhood home was, I do not know where she went to elementary school, although my father suggests Hamilton Elementary and Villacresta, and mentions, in passing, that her parents didn't own a phone at that point. Her middle-school experience seems to be split between the rather similar-sounding Pikesville and Parkville, and Parkville, I believe, is where she went to high school. What I know about her schooling is through fiction. In the summer of 1988, when I was nine, I went to the cinema with my parents. My father took me to see *The Fox and the Hound*, which I believed at the time had been written by Peet, although he had left the Disney umbrella almost twenty years before that film's initial release, as he details in his strange, bitter, beautifully illustrated autobiography. My mother went to a simultaneous showing of John Waters's film *Hairspray*. The Disney ended earlier, and so my father and I joined my mother in the cinema for the final moments of her film. She was the only audience member that day, and I stood at the back for a moment, watching her singing and waving her arms in the air, utterly enraptured, utterly unashamed. And after the film ended my mother said that this, this had been her high school, this had been her life.

It wasn't, as far as I can see, or not exactly. The Corny Collins Dance Show that is the centre of the film is based on the very real, rather peculiar, *Buddy Deane Show*; as Waters explains in a piece for *Baltimore* magazine published in April 1985, the show was 'a teenage dance party, on the air from 1957 to 1964' that was not only the top-rated local TV show in Baltimore but, briefly, the top-rated local TV show anywhere in the country. Waters focuses on the personalities of the teenage dancers and their hair, the influence of which, he notes, still lingers on in the 'great Hairdo Capital of the World'. The last of the *Buddy Deane* superstar dancers was one Mary Lou Raines, a fourteen-year-old Pimlico Junior High School student – could my mother have gone to Pimlico, rather than Parkville or Pikesville, I wonder – whose hairstyles included the Double Bubble, the Airlift, and, most intriguingly, the Artichoke.

The show came to an end because of its failure to integrate its dancers successfully; although the programme was essential in introducing white teenagers to Black music, and the show had one all-Black episode a month, protests for integration, largely originated by the NAACP, were met with threats and bomb scares, and the show was cancelled, a far unhappier end than Waters presents in *Hairspray* itself. A *Washington Post* piece published after Buddy Deane's death in 2003 notes that the segregationist policies of the show had long been condemned; the Baltimore City Board of Education withdrew support as early as 1958. A single integrated episode on 12 August 1963, arranged by a civil rights organisation called BAYOU (Baltimore Youth Opportunities Unlimited), led the show's producers to believe that while their teenage audience would probably support integration, their parents would not.

Given the show's popularity, it is very likely that she watched it. Given that it ended when she was nine, it is very unlikely that she knew any of the dancers, at least when it was on air. As the show recruited from across Baltimore city, there seems to be no particular reason why she saw a personal connection with the film, although there may be one. But what mattered more than anything, I think, was that Ruth Brown, the great soul singer, was cast in the film as Motormouth Maybelle, and Brown was one of the singers my mother, much later, would emulate. Because my mother could sing soul. Mainly Janis Joplin, a little Irma Thomas, but oh, she could belt it out, all the pain, all the joy, from the confines of her kitchen, wherever it was. Years later I would see the Aretha Franklin concert film *Amazing Grace*, and I would start to cry just moments in, because there was my mother, completely unexpectedly. In that film Aretha barely speaks – just a few words at the very end, and you see the men of the church, not least her father, speak for her, position her, hold her upright and hold her back. But oh, when she sings, the heavens break open, and the world is changed. But then, I see my mother everywhere, in every piece of art, in every song and every story. And I think she saw herself everywhere, too. Putting herself in other people's stories was a way of choosing a story that was less painful than her own. *Hairspray* was a way of giving her a voice, of representing not, perhaps, her own experiences, but her imagined ones, and they were as real, as necessary, as whatever truth of her past she might have known.

Waters was, indeed, often used for explanatory purposes. My mother often pointed to his later, more popular films as representing her childhood in the old, weird Baltimore. *Serial Mom*, notably, has a scene in which a police radio reports that Kathleen Turner is fleeing through Catonsville, the streets I grew up on, although the itinerary doesn't make a great deal of sense. My mother's over-identification with Turner's character worries me, a little. But my mother used to insist, in later years when I'd forgotten much of Baltimore, that she was from the Baltimore of John Waters, and my father from the Baltimore of Anne Tyler – indeed, *The Accidental Tourist* is set perhaps a block from my father's childhood home – and that this would explain things. And yet my father's brother's first date with a girl, family legend has it, was to one of Waters's earliest avant-garde films, screened in a church basement; he attended with his mother in tow, and so upsetting was the experience that it was to be some years before he went on a date with a girl again. This story is so improbable that I dearly want to believe it.

My childhood Baltimore was built from Bill Peet and L. Frank Baum, then, my mother's reconstructed by John Waters, both of us pulling from whatever sources we had to hand, constructing a world that felt suitable, that could explain something about ourselves, that we could tell ourselves and others as if repetition were a form of truth. I am happy to picture my mother in a world of teenage dance sensations and pop music – although her teenage fixations were directed much more closely to Peter Tork of the Monkees – and to skip over any literal truth.

And yet it is still odd to me that I would remember reading the Oz books. The stories are famous, because of the film, as declarations of a love of home. *The Wizard of Oz* itself is positioned as a story of adventure, yes, but more importantly as one of return. As a child I believed that films were shot sequentially, and that colour photography was invented on the day they began shooting the Oz sequence, and so I could never make much sense of the return to Kansas at the end. The identification scene – and you were there, and you were there – indicated less that Oz had been imagined than that the world was filled with uncanny doubles, and Kansas, after all, did not look appealing. I never much liked the book; Baum's writing was too fantastical, it moved too quickly, it introduced such odd ideas and characters without pausing to give them emotional weight. And *The Wonderful Wizard of Oz* is a book that cannot be read without overlaying the film on top of it; finding at the end that the Cowardly Lion's great victory is the killing of a giant spider seems improbable simply because it does not accord with the film.

Dorothy's return to Oz in the third volume, *Ozma of Oz*, the one I remember reading on that summer day, demonstrates that ideas of home are not overly central to Baum's imagination. Dorothy begins the story on a voyage to Australia with her uncle. Swept overboard in a storm, much like the Pevensie children, along with their odious cousin Eustace Clarence Scrubb, would be at the opening of *The Voyage of the Dawn Treader* some years later, she takes refuge on a floating chicken coop and, alongside a hen named Bill, she finds herself in the Land of Ev. The first sign that something fantastical has happened is Bill's discovery of language: Bill remarks that she's ' "clucked and cackled all my life, and never spoken a word before this morning" '. Dorothy promptly renames her Billina, as a name more fitting for a hen. As in the second book, *The Marvelous Land of Oz*, where the young protagonist, the orphan boy Tip, is discovered in fact to be Queen Ozma, Baum's representation of gender identity is surprisingly fluid. While the rest of the novel is filled with strange people – the Wheelers, who have wheels in place of their hands and feet, or the royal family of Ev, who have been transformed into decorative ornaments by the Nome King, or Princess Langwidere, who has a collection of thirty detachable heads which she alternates – Bill, or Billina, is perhaps the closest to an identificatory figure the young reader might find in the novel, as she is, in the end, a hen much like any other, save for her gift of speech. If everyone else is in a state of continual, often upsetting transformation, the chicken is the moral centre of the novel.

Billina, or Bill, is introduced as a sceptic, wondering how anyone could expect her to believe ' "impossible stories about animals that can talk" ' despite, of course, speaking herself. She clings to the name of Bill, despite Dorothy's admonishments, and consorts, or fights, with 'common chickens'. While Dorothy does return to her family in a three-sentence fragment at the novel's end, there is little sense, throughout the novel, that this represents the fulfilment of any deep longing. Instead it is Bill who most clearly occupies the figure of the rational, adult observer, at times even occupying a maternal role as she advises Dorothy about her diet. Even as she refuses to return to the ' "stupid, humdrum world" ' of the reader's own reality, Bill's decision to remain in Oz is based simply on the flavour of the insects there. If Dorothy flits between worlds, never fully settling anywhere, Bill learns to appreciate the world around her for whatever it can offer, and ignore its more fantastical elements.

Perhaps it's wrong, somehow, to read the Oz stories for the chickens. But there must be a reason that Merle, and Billina, are the figures I remember reading about. If nonhuman animals did not teach me how to share, if they were not moral exemplars, they were still figures of stability, of quietness, in a world where everything else seemed liable to fall into chaos. There is no greater privilege, and there are few greater needs, than to construct your own world, to find a place of stasis. If my mother needed to escape her past, I simply needed to know that it was certain, and this I learned from animals.

Charlotte's Web

The year after I read the Oz novels, when I was seven, we moved to Vermont, although it was to be some years before I wholly understood why. The initial impetus for the move was the presence of a particular church in the town of Putney, a Brethren parish headed by three pastors who lived, with their families, together in an enormous house; when my parents were unable to find a home nearby they opted for the next town over, by the singularly unlovely name of Dummerston, outside the larger town of Brattleboro, in the south-eastern corner of the state. The house they found had originally, in the nineteenth century, been the servants' quarters for the larger house next door, and had most recently been inhabited by a farming family, with cows pastured in the backyard. That family seemed to have left in something of a hurry. Bottles of milk, long since curdled, were still on the kitchen table when we viewed the house, the realtor having broken in by using a credit card to fiddle with the lock. Newspapers and magazines were stacked carefully enough that one could move from room to room along narrow paths, but neither floors nor walls were visible, only a miasma of grime and rural poverty. In some rooms the holes in the floor were simply obscured by piles of papers, or old furniture. My father paid cash, a piddling sum, no doubt to the great relief of the realtor.

At my paternal grandfather's funeral, many years later, my grandmother gave me a packet of photos my mother had sent them a year or two after the move. I suppose I should find in them a record of a rural idyll, the one that I remember from that time, where if I wasn't playing with, or herding, the sheep and goats and chickens we kept, I was alone in the neighbouring woods, a stretch of a hundred acres – how very A. A. Milne – mainly kept for logging, filled with streams to be dammed and rocks to climb. It was the sort of childhood many people might envision stopped being possible a century ago. But the photos tell a different story; while I understand, now, the humour in sending relatives a picture of a hen poking its head out of a rotting pumpkin – an image central, curiously, to the film *Return to Oz*, an adaptation of *Ozma* that I didn't see until I was forty, but in which Bill is every bit as central as in the novel – at first glance the pictures seem bare and dreary. Two images of our house, taken to show the multi-foot icicles dangling from the eaves, highlight instead how urgently in need of painting it is. The photobook is strangely desolate, resistant to nostalgia.

Of the twenty-four photos in this little book – the most extensive photographic record I now have of my childhood, the family photo albums having been mysteriously lost after my mother's death, and presumably now sitting in an attic or basement, but never found in fifteen years of searching – only three were taken by someone other than one of my parents, probably my father: a school photo from September 1987, which I remember vividly because I somehow forgot to wear my glasses and worried I would not be recognisable, and two earlier photos from my grandparents' house in Baltimore, where my father seems to be analysing some sort of paperwork under his parents' supervision, while I lurk in the corner, wearing a Groucho Marx nose and holding an enormous magnifying glass, no doubt trying to emulate Sherlock Holmes.

Of the fifteen remaining photographs that include animals or people, I appear in six, while nine feature only pets or livestock. In a Christmas sequence I appear alone on the floor underneath a straggly tree, chopped down in the woods by my father a few days earlier; I look excited, then happy, then somewhat overwhelmed. A fluffy black-and-white cat whose name I cannot remember watches over me, as do a stuffed pig, its fur worn smooth, called Bacon and my Cabbage Patch Doll, named Eustace, after Clarence Scrubb. Narnia references abound; a cat, surprisingly beautiful, named Rilian sits in the nook of an enormous German tile stove, also surprisingly beautiful, built by my father, while one of the goats is my own special pet, Digory. There are only two photos that show my parents, however.

One shows a scene in the woods: the photograph is so under-exposed that only a sapling in the right foreground is clearly visible. I am walking along a path in the upper-left corner of the frame; I know it is me because of the top I am wearing, which is revealed in the following pictures to be a t-shirt that reads 'Vermont: our kids run wild' with a picture of a goat. Next to me is a taller figure, wearing a t-shirt and jeans, but a shaft of light blots out the figure's head. I suspect, by stance, that this must be my father; my mother might be somewhere behind us, behind the camera, watching us walk away. The image has not turned sepia, but simply grey, and the human figures are miniscule in comparison to the swathes of undifferentiated trees that dominate the image.

The other is clearly taken by my father; it seems that I've inherited his tendency to line a tree up on one side of the photograph as an internal frame. It shows the whole of our house, and is taken from the road, near the communal postboxes on the corner where two roads met, beneath the shade of a giant catalpa tree. Two sheep graze in the front yard, although there is no sign of fencing, and little for them to eat; the locust and catalpa trees in front of the house have no leaves, although neither is there any snow, so it must be early spring. To the right of the house there is a canoe and a small woodpile. To the left you can see a bird feeder perched on a fencepost, and around ten chickens scrabbling in the dirt. Behind them, almost invisible, is my mother. She is obscured by the corner of the house, and is standing with her hands in her pockets; the image is too small for me to see her face, but her stance is sceptical. Her hair is longer than I remember it being, she is wearing jeans, but otherwise it is too indistinct for me to make out more.

If this picture was taken in 1987, or possibly 1988, my mother is somewhere between thirty-two and thirty-four years old. She would live, at most, for another eighteen years. This is the most recent picture of her I own. And I cannot see her.

I was bafflingly angry at my mother when she died for being so camera-shy, despite my own lifelong resistance to having my photo taken. In a family of three, it seems cruel that there were almost no family photos, much less the videos that every other person of my generation seemed to acquire. The only photo I have of the three of us sits on my office desk now; it was taken sometime early in 1979, as I might be a month or two old. The photo, originally black-and-white, has gone slightly green, but my parents are radiant. My father, in ponytail, open-necked shirt, and a surpassingly cool black jacket, looks only at my mother, despite holding me, a giant smile on his face. My mother's smile is more shy; her eyes are mostly closed, but she is looking neither quite at my father nor at me nor the unknown photographer, but seems lost in a world of her own. I look like a baby, much like any other. But they look untroubled, unworried, sufficient in themselves. They look deeply in love.

There are, perhaps, many reasons my mother refused to have her photo taken for the majority of her life. I doubt that her parents took many of her; my father reports that her grandmother lived down the street from them when my mother was a child, and would come into their house and cut my mother's face out of any photos she could find. I do not know why. When my parents fell in love and wanted to get married, perilously young, there was discussion of getting the law involved, and a photographic record might have been harmful. By the time I knew her my mother's body was damaged by years of prescription steroids, mainly prednisone taken as an immunosuppressant, and she felt ungainly, stranded in a body that was not hers. And yet. I am happy to have these pictures of goats and sheep and chickens and dogs and cats, and, in truth, they were as much a part of my everyday family as my parents, but I have never stopped wanting to see my parents' faces.

My mother gave me a book, once, as explanation. Randall Jarrell's *The Animal Family* is a small book, quite literally, square in shape and with enormous margins, so that a small block of text occupies less than half of each page. The seven illustrations by Maurice Sendak, placed at the beginning of each chapter, strike me as some of his finest pen-and-ink work; they are carefully, intricately constructed, and much larger than the surrounding text. They depict not characters but settings: the woods, the sea, a tree. Jarrell's story is simple. A hunter lives alone; he meets, and falls in love with, a mermaid; he brings home a little bear to be their child, and then a lynx, and then a human baby. The animals do not speak, while the hunter speaks rarely; the little dialogue in the book is primarily spoken by the mermaid, expressing her confusion at her new home on land. The style is austere, unromanticised. Each character is complete in themselves: as much as they complement each other, they are marked as individuals with separate desires. It is only the arrival of the human child that makes them coalesce into a family. In the book's final lines, the hunter and mermaid speak to their son, and begin 'their old game' of pretending not to have found him alone on the beach: ' "We've had you always", says the mermaid.

Jarrell's story is simple precisely because it is so very complicated. Family, he suggests, does not require causation, or chronology, or blood. It is not built wholly on romance, or plans for the future. Family is the coming together of individuals, by their own independent choice. It is not a given form of belonging, but a chosen one.

And this was my family too, an organisation of choice as much as necessity, a grouping that seemed set against the world, that thrived in isolation. A family that made little space for blood ties, but plenty for goats. It was, for a moment, the family my mother wanted.

That year we cut off the last threads of communication with my mothers' parents; I did not speak with them again before their deaths, although every few months, for many years, I would search the internet for their obituaries, until at last I found them. The last time I saw my maternal grandmother she bent down to kiss me, and I recoiled; I ran into the house and put the original cast recording of *Peter Pan* on as loud as I could, Mary Martin singing 'I've Gotta Crow' at the top of her lungs. I never looked back. Relations with my father's family were intermittent – phone calls every few months, a fleeting visit every few years – but rare. And yet my mother was not wholly alone; there were connections to other farmers, other craftspeople, congregants in the various churches we attended, the occasional birthday party with my classmates. There were nearby neighbours to the west and east. But the pre-dominant memory is of a family of three humans and many other animals, poised against the rest of the world. In this choice, in this poise, I have to believe my mother was at her happiest.

The economist Robert Urquhart, who briefly cites Jarrell's story in his book *Ordinary Choices*, looks at the tradition of French phenomenology following Maurice Merleau-Ponty to argue that every choice we make starts with how the world actually appears to us. We do not choose in the abstract, but in the immediate, sensory, and sensual world. And that choice is important because it is what marks us as individuals, and allows us to recognise others as individuals. We do not begin with theories, or with quantitative data; we begin with our own immediate, bodily experience of the world and the things around us. The world, he says, is the 'field for our ordinary experience', an experience which requires that we 'live among others whom we must accept and take seriously as having their own independent existence'. And this was my mother's practice: everything can be chosen, every choice grants agency, every choice places you as an individual among other individuals.

Sometimes she argued that this was a belief born of theology, especially the mystics she loved so dearly, from Julian of Norwich to Thomas Merton; sometimes she framed it as her own response to second-wave feminism. But there was never a question that family, that any mode of interpersonal relations, was always a choice. Nothing was owed, nothing was predetermined.

As Dot sings in Stephen Sondheim's *Sunday in the Park with George*, which became my favourite musical when I first heard it at thirteen, and has remained so ever since: 'The choice may have been mistaken / The choosing was not'. In his discussion of the song 'Move On' from which the line comes, Sondheim quotes the French poet Paul Valéry's aphorism that a poem is never finished, only abandoned.

I think we could say the same for our lives: never finished, only abandoned. But we choose, even when we don't think we have a choice.

The Animal Family was published when my mother was ten, and perhaps she read it at that time, perhaps later. When I first read it, though, it did not seem explanatory, simply familiar. I already knew that families were comprised of individual choice. Likewise, I read through the works of Laura Ingalls Wilder several times over, but found nothing exceptional in them; we too lived in a little house in the big woods, and nothing much had changed, except that we, at least, had a shortwave radio that we listened to in the evenings, mainly BBC radio dramas.

Instead, I found a framework for my experience in the story of a pig.

E.B. White's *Charlotte's Web* does not have a particular setting, although it seems likely it is based in a town not unlike that of White's Maine home. In the 1973 animated adaptation, however, there is a very brief scene in the farmyard where a newspaper blows past, and for a moment you can see its name, the *Brattleboro Prattle*. There is only one Brattleboro in the world, with a newspaper called the *Brattleboro Reformer*, and this was my own local newspaper – and, indeed, one my parents had subscribed to when we lived in Baltimore, thanks to its relatively radical politics. There is nothing else in the film to suggest a Vermont setting, and I have no doubt that the name was chosen simply for its comic sound, and yet, there I am, in passing, the same way I find myself inscribed on Merle's tree. If you look hard enough, you can convince yourself that every story is about you.

The farm in White's novel is a bit larger than ours was, the children a bit better adjusted, and we had no pigs. Ours was a fantasy of a farm, more than a farm itself. My mother had designed a name – Little Flock Farm – and a logo, but the farm, such as it was, was more constructed from a general back-to-the-land ethos than much contemporary farming knowledge, although my father studied agriculture during the two years he spent at university in Iowa, and had kept many of his textbooks. Our farm equipment mainly came from the local auction house; the hay was hand-scythed, rather than mown; the barn, when my father built it, was framed and then put into place with an old-fashioned barn raising; the shearers who came for the sheep used hand-shears, and told me about Thornton Wilder and William Saroyan. My mother preserved vegetables and spun wool, and my parents invested in a giant treadle loom, although used it only briefly. It was a product of idealism as much as practical knowledge; if it provided almost enough food for us to live on, it never turned, nor was intended to turn, a profit.

White's farm is, perhaps, more up-to-date than my own, despite *Charlotte's Web* being published three decades before my parents' own agricultural adventures. The story is as moving as you remember, and probably a bit better written than you noticed. It opens, famously, with the threat of death, as spoken by an uncomprehending child: ' "Where's Papa going with that axe?" ' Untimely violent death is always imminent, and as much as the reader sympathises with the child Fern's desire to save the pig Wilbur, there is no sense that a peaceful end for Wilbur will become the new status quo.

This sense of exceptionalism is present in almost every farmyard story: the reader roots for one particular animal not to be eaten, but never challenges the idea that pigs and other livestock are, in general, to be eaten. This is what the critic Amy Ratelle calls the 'civilizing process' common to children's animal literature, where the child reader first learns to empathise with the animal characters, but then learns to position themselves outside that dynamic. Wilbur's fear of death is real and visceral, but the novel does not, perhaps, make vegetarians of many of its readers.

This failure of expansion, however, is also the core of the story, and why, perhaps, White's novel holds up better than similarly themed tales. The humans in the story think that Wilbur is an exceptional pig, and they think this because they are told that he is by the spider Charlotte. When Charlotte spins her first message, 'Some pig', the farmer Mr Zuckerman immediately reports that Wilbur is extraordinary, although in what way he doesn't know. His wife cautions him that they might have an unusual spider, not an unusual pig, but her doubt is not repeated by any of the other human characters; Wilbur has been pronounced as special, and so he must be. White's satire of the PR and advertising industry is funnier, and more cutting, than I remember.

Although Wilbur, in his innate goodness, innocence, and loneliness, is easily the reader surrogate in the text, Fern's own conversations with animals represents how a child reader might want to envision themselves. Her father assuages fears that Fern may have an overactive imagination with the sentiment that maybe adult ears simply aren't as finely attuned to animal speech as those of children. Part of what makes *Charlotte's Web* so remarkable is that while it bears the earmarks of fantasy, talking animals and all, it is neither rigidly in the world of the fantastic, like White's *Stuart Little*, nor quite as surreal as his novel *The Trumpet of the Swan*. Even now I cannot come to terms with the latter book, in which a voiceless trumpeter swan named Louis learns to write on a chalkboard, and then play the trumpet, as alternate forms of communication; while his actions are out of love for a female swan named Serena, notably absent from most of the story, it is a strangely lonely book. Louis is isolated from his swan family, both his mother's silent worry and his father's endless verbosity. He is transfigured into something other, even having the webs in his feet cut so that he can play the trumpet better. He is exploited by humans who only value him for the financial potential of his music. It reads to me now as an allegory for disability, or for queerness, and yet it returns again and again to a normalised, conservative conception of the world. It incorporates fairly realistic pen-and-ink descriptions with hand-drawn sheet music; it is poetic and comic and remarkably unsettling.

Charlotte's Web, however, is so well grounded, so recognisable in its specifics, that it's easy to believe that, if we just listened harder, this is what we might hear. As a child I was just as fond of Walter R. Brooks's Freddy the Pig stories, a twenty-six-book series describing the increasingly silly adventures of a set of farmyard animals much like the ones White describes. Going back to them now, however, I find that the characters are simply too anthropomorphised. In *Freddy the Detective*, the third in the series, Freddy the Pig is inspired to become a detective after reading a series of Sherlock Holmes stories, but is initially frustrated because the specifics of those stories are so different from his own environment. He does, of course, find and solve a great mystery, and justice is served at the end, and yet the explicit mapping of human constructs onto animal characters remains dissatisfying. Brooks – who, as it turns out, also created Mister Ed, the talking horse – moves too far into the realm of the fantastic, so that the animality of his protagonists is ultimately beside the point. White's novel, however, presents not a world of the imagination so much as a world of potential, of possibility, of belonging. For the reader, as for Wilbur, the world is bewildering and threatening, but if we listen closely, if we pay attention, if we base our choices in our own immediate experience, we can find a form of acceptance, of family.

And that acceptance is rooted in the proximity of death. One of Wilbur's early conversations with Charlotte, and the genesis of her plan, is when he whispers to her of his own death, beginning to 'tremble with fear' like a porcine Kierkegaard. He doesn't want to die, he says, he wants to stay in the barn; ' "Of course" ', responds

Charlotte, ' "we all do" '. If Wilbur's potential death is the narrative centre of the novel, and Charlotte's actual death its emotional centre, White insists that these deaths are not exceptional; death is what marks us as individual, what gives shape to our lives. It is precisely because death is universal that it matters so much to us as individuals, that it seems so much like a rupture. Even the summer, the crickets sing, is dying.

The older reader, no doubt, realises that Charlotte will die long before the child reader does, and certainly long before Wilbur. What makes *Charlotte's Web* so different from *The Story of Babar*, or even *Bambi*, is that while the maternal figure dies in all of them, in White's novel it is not a surprise, but simply muted; Charlotte says only that she is 'languishing', and Wilbur occasionally notices the sadness in her voice, but her death is neither violent nor unexpected. Structurally, too, the death of a parent in many other texts, and indeed films, is used as a catalyst for the development of the protagonist, coming at the beginning. Here, though, it comes near the end, when Wilbur has already grown into a knowledge and love of the world.

And it is no less moving for that. Charlotte's final set of speeches, where she explains her death, is grounded in her own acceptance of her fate: ' "what's a life, anyway?" ' she asks. Helping others, bringing them into the world, becomes a way of elevating her own brief existence. There are shades of more sentimental, and crueller, children's stories here, such as Shel Silverstein's abominable *The Giving Tree*, where a tree – feminised, of course – gives every part of herself to the protagonist, until she dies, because love, it seems, is only in sacrifice. And yet although Charlotte has sacrificed something of herself, she is not defined by that sacrifice, but by her choice to create, to produce something new, to invest herself in the lives of others.

Charlotte's death haunts us, or haunts me, because it is the death of an individual, rather than someone living out a preordained role. She is mother and friend at the same time, and not restricted to either category. She saves Wilbur simply because she can. And she saves him to preserve not one pig, but the entire world. She tells Wilbur about the beauties of winter and spring to come, all the joys of the world, which she cannot partake in. Because the chapter is titled 'Last Day', this final conversation seems clear, and yet the reader is unprepared for the shock of the final sentence: 'No one was with her when she died.' Of course, we insist, someone should be with her; Charlotte has been such a great friend that she should receive friendship in return, some comfort. And yet she is alone.

But this is the trick of White's book, and perhaps all books, because Charlotte is not alone. It is not only that she lives on, in the novel's final chapters, in memory and story, that her children learn about her and learn to love her memory, to love what White calls simply 'the glory of everything'. It is that we, the readers, are with her when she dies. She is not unseen, she is not unmourned, because we are at her side. We love her, and it is a real love. There is loss, but there is also incorporation; Charlotte's story, her life, becomes part of us, and we, through it, move into that love of the world.

Earlier in the novel, a passage where Wilbur becomes aware of his impending death is introduced with a lengthy, sensual description of a single evening.

Twilight settled over Zuckerman's barn, and a feeling of peace. Fern knew it was almost supper-time but she couldn't bear to leave. Swallows passed on silent wings, in and out of the doorways, bringing food to their young ones. From across the road a bird sang 'Whippoorwill, whippoorwill!' Lurvy sat down under an apple tree and lit his pipe: the animals sniffed the familiar smell of strong tobacco. Wilbur heard the trill of the tree toad and the occasional slamming of the kitchen door. All these sounds made him feel comfortable and happy, for he loved life and loved to be a part of the world on a summer evening. But as he lay there he remembered what the old sheep had told him. The thought of death came to him and he began to tremble with fear.

The temptation is to skip to the end of the paragraph, because this is where our plot, and our emotional involvement, is centred. And yet the time White takes to describe this ordinary evening is just as important. The moment is experienced through all the senses, and by a multitude of different creatures. To love the world means to be wholly embedded in it, entangled with other living beings. It is only because we love the world that we fear death.

But it is also just as much because we fear death that we tell stories. It is storytelling, White insists, as much as Lobel or Minarik or Peet, that allows this sense of embeddedness, this sense of life. Charlotte matters because she tells stories about, and to, Wilbur, and because Wilbur then tells stories about her to her children. Stories are what let us transcend our individuality; they are the part of us that matters.

There is so much in *Charlotte's Web* that shouldn't work: the combination of irony and sentiment, the threat and comfort, the loss and the love. And yet White insists that we must begin with the world as it is. We must begin with the idea that the world is cruel, that it is confusing, that it can so easily be misperceived. And from that we choose the life we want to lead, the people we want to be, a choice we make in the face of our own death, and the deaths of those we love. And from that moment, we learn how beautiful the world is, that there is a story of which we are part, and that even when we are gone, that story will endure.

The Wind in the Willows

All childhood is an imagined world. It's rare to find a memoir of childhood reading that does not begin with, or at least include, a love of maps. The places of fiction define and extend our own. Alison Bechdel, in her graphic memoir (or 'tragicomic') *Fun Home*, provides several maps of her childhood home in Pennsylvania, some topographic and some more schematic, illustrating natural and built features, and the relation between various family members. The most complete map, showing almost the whole town, occupies the lower half of a page, two-thirds of the way through the book. The top half of the page is a reproduction of the map from Kenneth Grahame's *The Wind in the Willows*; Bechdel mentions taking it from a colouring book, although it is almost identical to the endpapers of my own edition of the novel, as illustrated by E. H. Shepherd. Bechdel has carefully, accurately redrawn the map, making some of its features more clear. The visual parallels between the two maps are obvious, but Bechdel articulates them all the same; the maps show the same iron bridge, the same ford, the same area filled with weasels and stoats, or people Bechdel's family disliked. But on the facing page she presents the map again, closer-up, pointing out that if you look closely enough, you can see Mr Toad driving along in his motorcar. And she's right; going back to my own volume, if I look very closely there he is, something I had never noticed in all my years of reading Grahame's novel. For Bechdel this has a particular significance: the road where Mr Toad is driving is paralleled by the road where, years later, her father will be hit by a truck, one of the traumas that underpins her text. But she also points out that there is life, animation, within the map. Maps are not static: they tell their own stories and ours, too.

Far more than the picture-books I read a few years earlier, or even Oz, *The Wind in the Willows* provides a map for, it seems, a great many child readers. In Lynda Barry's own graphic memoir *One! Hundred! Demons!* she laments, at the very end, that she worried she could never become a writer because she didn't know Grahame's text, and seemingly every other writer did. Lucy Mangan, in *Bookworm*, her memoir of childhood reading, describes herself as an 'idiot' for ruling out Grahame's work, along with every other talking animal story. But for so many others, adults and children, ever since its initial publication, *The Wind in the Willows* is not just a shared reading experience, but a shared place. In a frequently cited letter from January 1909, Theodore Roosevelt writes, on White House stationery, that he feels much the same about going to Africa as the seafaring rat feels when he describes his travels. And those of us less entranced by mass slaughter and colonialisation might feel similarly. Our ideas of life on a river, or on the road, or in a wonderful hole in the ground or a great manor, all seem to stem from this novel. It is familiar and foreign at the same time; Grahame writes of a vanished world, a pastoral idyll that may never have existed, in which the details are both implausible and tangible.

For the surprising thing about *The Wind in the Willows* is the problem of scale. That smaller animals – toads and water rats and moles – might consort with slightly larger animals such as badgers seems perfectly plausible. That each of our main characters is known by species seems a bit odd – surely there must have been a mole mother and a mole father, a neighbouring rat? – but this is not wholly unusual, and leads to Mole's great war-cry, 'A Mole! A Mole!', which is probably my favourite moment in the book, although my father would no doubt go for the phrase 'whack 'em and whack 'em and whack 'em', which was something of a family mantra, even if there was never a particular 'them' to whack. But that toads can drive fancy cars, that toads and moles can both wear the clothing of washerwomen, that weasels can carry what appear to be full-sized weapons – this is not only difficult to justify with our know-ledge of animal lives, but challenges our very understanding of the animals' physical size. The relation between animals and humans in the novel is similarly complex: in a brief, almost dys-topian moment Grahame mentions that the Wild Wood is on the site of a prior human civilisation, as humans are more likely to vanish from a place than the animals, and yet there are certainly many humans in the novel. The humans keep animals as pets, as the discovery of a bird in a cage reveals, and yet are not terribly surprised to find themselves in conversation with animals either, treating them almost as equals. The rules of the novel are strangely inconsistent: if Mole is large enough to wear human clothing, his hole in the ground must itself be relatively large, and yet there is no suggestion that it is. There are just enough indications that our protagonists are animals that we must, in reading, take it seriously, and yet there is, for much of the novel, no reason to think of them as anything other than human.

And the glory of the novel, of course, is that it doesn't matter. It isn't simply that we take the driving abilities of toads seriously, but that we accept whatever is on the page in front of us, without wondering for very long how it accords with what we found a few pages before. And this is just as true as the narrative overall. Many readers will remember the story of Mr Toad and his adven-tures, some will remember the far more affecting scenes with Rat, Toad, and Badger, but few might remember the mystical vision of Pan, or the chapter devoted to the unnamed seafaring rat who inspires reveries in Rat himself, the final two episodes of the novel to be written, and perhaps the most beautiful. *The Wind in the Willows* is a curious text to reread, because parts of it seem as if we've always known them, and parts seem wholly new to us. What we might remember as a story, a narrative, turns out to be a series of fragments.

It is the same with our own lives, of course. We remember, or think we remember, a story, a progression that takes us from where we were to where we are now. But however hard we look, we find only pieces that refuse to cohere.

The act of rereading, as many critics have noted, evokes two readers: the one who is reading the work and the one who read it first, what Wendy Lesser, in *Nothing Remains the Same*, calls 'a little reflected face' of 'the person you were when you first read the book'. Revisiting the books we read in childhood is a way of revisiting our childhood selves. Often this provides a sense of continuity; we may be charmed to find ourselves moved by a text in the same way, we may be delighted that our taste in fiction then accords with our taste in fiction now. We might be surprised to find that a text informed the way we see the world to such an extent. I read *The Hobbit*, as I've said, every three months as a child, and then didn't read it for a decade, and returning to it one gloomy day at university I was shocked to realise how many stories there were in it; it had filled my memory so comprehensively that I couldn't quite understand how so many characters and set-pieces all fit within several hundred pages. Surely the adventures in Mirkwood, so rich in my imagination, must have required a novel of their own, and couldn't be part of the same story as Bilbo's later encounters with Smaug.

And of course the opposite is just as true. We might be baffled that we enjoyed a text we now see as mediocre. We might worry at how poorly our childhood reading reflected the diversity of the world, and wonder what that might say about us. We might find ourselves faced with moments of discomfort, wondering how much the orthodoxies of the past affected our own way of seeing the world. We might take the opportunity to praise our intellectual superiority in the present, out of some deeply misplaced sense of competition with our former selves. Sometimes, in assembling these fragments, I've returned to a much-loved text from childhood and been entirely unable to understand what made me love it years ago. Books that once seemed rich and full now seem flat, didactic, undeveloped.

But rereading is far more than this tension between continuity and discontinuity, or between stability and change, as Patricia Meyer Spacks frames it in her book *On Rereading*, for we read not simply as adult and child selves, isolated from the world, but as people who have been enmeshed in it, who have had other experiences, who have read other books. The critic Matei Călinescu uses the term 'circular haunting' to describe this potential paradox. No book, he says, is encountered on its own. We always read through the prism of the other books we've read, the lives we've lived. And when we reread, our own act of reading becomes such a prism. It is not simply that we cannot go back to a text as if for the first time; it is that that first reading, and everything we have read since, informs our rereading, and the rereading changes how we remember the first reading. I cannot read *The Hobbit* now without adding to it my memories of reading *The Lord of the Rings*, of seeing the film of *The Return of the King* in the cinema on a Christmas morning and sobbing with relief that it had been released before my mother died. All of those experiences are now part of the original. To misquote Heraclitus, you cannot read the same book twice. While Spacks argues that rereading childhood books often invokes a sense of nostalgia, a moment of being able to be swept back into a familiar world, we are also always haunted by the sense that not only have we changed, but the book itself is rendered different just by the fact that we, now, are rereading it.

And this dual sense of permanence and change is one of the glories of *The Wind in the Willows*, a book that is not, perhaps, about rereading, but is about how we revisit the places we love, and find them strange, yet no less longed for. The novel, you'll recall, opens with change. The Mole is cleaning his house, and as much as he cleans, he feels himself called by something else, a sense of adventure borne in the spring air, and so he departs. Indeed, he 'scrooges' out of his hole, and if we have since read Dickens, we bring a set of associations to the word we did not previously have. And he goes to the river, and to the world.

For this is not only a story of leave-taking, but homecoming. Four chapters later Mole comes home, and, unlike Toad, he does not compose a song about it. Mole and Rat pass by Mole's home, and he is filled, in one of the most emotionally charged scenes in the book, with an indescribable longing. Grahame's narrator laments that, as humans, we do not have the sense of 'intercommunication' with a place that the Mole has. But oh, it rends my heart. I know this loss, this sense of expulsion from the world, this feeling that wherever one is, one must be homesick. And his home, Grahame says, is also mole-sick. His home, thinks Mole, is shabby, and yet he had been happy there, and even more, his home had itself been happy, and it misses him. It is not only Mole who longs for home, but his home that longs for him, a true companionship.

And he tries to resist, he really does. He walks past, he holds firm, he refuses to explain himself to Rat, but finally, in a violent 'paroxysm of grief' he admits his desire. And his home welcomes him in. He and Rat prepare food, and tidy, and welcome in carolling field mice, and domestic bliss is achieved.

There are many homes in the novel, from the grandeur of Toad Hall to the propriety of Badger's sett, but there is no more homely place than Mole's, for there the desire to inhabit and the desire to be inhabited comingle. The home and the dweller have a fully symbiotic relationship, in which each is complete only with the other.

And so it sometimes is with our rereading. We pass over a book we once knew well, and we are sure that we have moved on in the world, that our new adventures are so much richer that this text cannot speak to us. And yet we cannot move forward. We are called back. And the book welcomes us in, and much has changed, and much has not. We are who we were when first we read the book, and who we are now, and we learn to embrace our own multiplicity, just as the book, if it's good enough, if it's true enough, embraces its own many readings. Grahame's novel, for all its episodic structure, is unified by a sense of constant yearning, a yearning for home and a yearning for away, and neither can quite be satiated and so we, too, yearn for the new and the familiar, always moving, always wishing to stay in place.

The critic James Wood adopts a word from Freud, 'afterwardness', to describe this phenomenon. The choices he made when young, the choice he made to leave his home, may not have seemed large at the time, and yet, he says, the 'process of retro-spective comprehension' that allows him to reflect on his leaving is what 'constitutes a life'. We cannot unmake our choices. We cannot go home. And we cannot, in the end, even know if our leave-taking was the right choice; it was simply the one we made. And yet that desire to go back, to look again, underpins all our self-comprehension. We are homesick not only for the places we left, but for the people we were when we left them. And this is the crux of rereading, too: it is not a form of nostalgia, but homesick-ness. It is a moment of afterwardness.

There were two giant willow trees outside our house in Dummer-ston, and a river at the bottom of the hill. One of my first jobs, alongside collecting rocks from the garden in five-gallon pails, at the rate of twenty-five cents a bucket, was the never-ending task of collecting the fallen willow twigs and burning them. But I preferred the river. It was no more than a stream, really, thin enough in summer heatwaves that you could easily step across it; it ran from the top of the wood to a neighbour's pond, and then slowly disappeared not too far down the road. And it was my river; it could easily be dammed or expanded, the contours shifting depending on my mood. Summer afternoons could be entirely occupied with considering how a particular bend in the river ought to appear. The woods were for family walks, and I rarely went more than a mile into them by myself; the apple orchards beyond were far more exotic (and did, indeed, some years later make their film debut in the adaptation of John Irving's *The Cider House Rules*). The closest I came to mischief as a child was going to the edge of the orchard with a childhood friend and stealing a fallen apple; it made me feel much more like Tom Sawyer than Saint Augustine. But the river was mine alone. Sometimes a chicken would get out of its coop and make its way down there, but otherwise, although I couldn't have been more than 500 feet from the house, it was a place of complete serenity, a place where I knew my world, and shaped it with my hands.

It always sounds like an exaggeration when I tell people that the Vermont part of my childhood was essentially set in the nineteenth century, and perhaps it is. We had electricity and running water (pumped from the stream). Since my father worked primarily on a barter system we had a chest freezer in which there would inevitably be half a pig or a cow that he had received in exchange for building a stone wall or a brick chimney. But it was extraordinarily, stereotypically, wilfully rustic. We had no television for the first few years – and when we did, it was a tiny black-and-white one that only received one station – and rarely went to town. The house was heated by wood, and only on the ground floor, so in the winter I would heat a stone by the fire to take upstairs to bed, and in the mornings the windows would be coated with ice. (The small fish in the aquarium I kept next to my bed did not fare well in such conditions.) We lived at the end of the power line, so every time it was windy we would fill the bath with water and read or play board games under the light of oil lamps, or I would card wool for my mother's spinning. It is, in some sense, little wonder that I would find more to recognise in Grahame – or, indeed, in the works of Laura Ingalls Wilder and L. M. Montgomery – than in Beverly Cleary or Judy Blume.

It is very easy to romanticise such a past. In my early teenage years I was desperate to leave – although not so desperate, it seems, that I ever learned to drive – and when I left at sixteen I suspected I would never come back for long. And yet years later, bringing my partner at the time to my father's wedding, staying in what used to be the cottage for migrant workers in the orchard – now operated as a holiday property by the National Trust, one of a small handful of properties they own in America, all close to my childhood home – I instantly thought 'and what a wonderful place to raise a child this must be.'

And like *Charlotte's Web*, this wonder at the world suffuses *The Wind in the Willows*. Some years after the novel's publication, and Grahame's death, his wife Elspeth published a small book, *First Whisper of The Wind in the Willows*, which includes some of the early letters Grahame wrote to his son Mouse (or Alastair) containing the story of Toad. The largest part of her introduction is given over to an appreciation of the novel from an American academic named Clayton Hamilton, who first tells the story of visiting a bookshop in New Mexico, finding a copy of the book there, and befriending the shopkeeper over their mutual love of Grahame's novel. Hamilton then quotes Grahame himself – although he acknowledges that he cannot report with 'absolute fidelity' – saying that 'The most priceless possession of the human race is the wonder of the world. Yet, latterly, the utmost endeavours of mankind have been directed towards the dissipation of that wonder.'

As an academic, I know perfectly well that this is not a reliable source. Elspeth's book is not taken seriously in academic circles. Grahame's biographer Matthew Dennison calls it a series of 'misleading, saccharine "memories"' that emphasise her own role in the novel's creation, and depict a far happier marriage than is generally agreed to have been the case. And yet while it is a strange text, it is also oddly moving. Much of the introduction is presented as a work of mourning: in bringing Mouse, styled here as 'the Listener', to the attention of the reading public Elspeth argues that the recipient of a story is as active in its creation as the storyteller. Alastair himself was not a happy child, and his death at twenty, an apparent suicide, colours Elspeth's memories of the stories themselves. It is the sort of story, I think, my mother would have told had I too taken my life at twenty, as I was so close to doing; in the following years she would say that keeping me alive was the hardest thing she had ever had to do. And if Elspeth feels, quite clearly, that she failed her son, in returning him to the story, in inserting women and children in a novel so completely concerned with the lives of middle-aged men, she tries to grant a permanence to the ephemeral, fleeting moments of connection in her own life. We must, she insists, reread this story in a new way now that we know that it was not a form of escape, but one of connection.

And so I want to believe her quotation of Hamilton, and his quotation of Grahame, knowing full well that this may only be a romanticisation of the past. Because the glory of the book is its poeticisation of the commonplace, its willingness to be, perhaps, overwritten, overly beautiful, to insist that every moment of experience carries meaning. And it is a resolutely textual world. Near the start of chapter 3, Mole thinks of his summer adventures with Rat, as recounted in the first two chapters.

Such a rich chapter it had been, when one came to look back on it all! With illustrations so numerous and so very highly coloured! The pageant of the river bank had marched steadily along, unfolding itself in scene-pictures that succeeded each other in stately procession. Purple loosestrife arrived early, shaking luxuriant tangled locks along the edge of the mirror whence its own face laughed back at it. Willow-herb, tender and wistful, like a pink sunset cloud, was not slow to follow. Comfrey, the purple hand-in-hand with the white, crept forth to take its place in the line; and at last one morning the diffident and delaying dog-rose stepped delicately on the stage, and one knew, as if string-music had announced it in stately chords that strayed into a gavotte, that June at last was here.

This story is a dance, a song, an illustration. As readers of more modern editions, we cannot help but see Shepherd's famous illustrations alluded to here, so numerous and highly coloured. The story of Mole is our own story. And yet this is not the story of Mole, but the story of the world. The flowers are just as important, and if the prose is, almost literally, purple, we can forgive Grahame this effusion, because every plant, every animal, every person has, he insists, a capacity for wonder. To look closely at the world is to see in it a story, a story that is played before us and yet in which we ourselves are participants.

And I see, in these very flowers, my own life played before me, a cat named Comfrey, the willows outside my house. I may not be able to recognise a dog-rose, but the name conjures up my first dog, Woodruff, named after the flowering shrub, and my first word (much to my mother's lifelong chagrin). I want to live in this world where each bloom is an adventure.

For reading the story now I cannot find myself particularly excited about the world of Toad. He is a tiresome sort of hero, and even as a child I could not understand why he would leave behind a perfectly satisfactory caravan for the thrill of a motor car. But I do want to live in a world where, if I listen hard enough, I can find Pan, with a lost baby otter nestled at his feet.

I struggle now, reading the novel, to come to terms with its social world. The novel does not merely depict a homosocial universe, but one predicated on gender and class assumptions that I repudiate; the only role available to women, besides some very unimportant mothers, is that of washerwoman, and there are few worse fates imaginable. The conservatism of Badger, which we seem meant to admire, and the flashy, carefree wealth of Toad, which is a bit more ambiguous, would both disturb me in some way if I encountered them now among human peers. And this unsettling preponderance of men, mostly white, mostly English, in my childhood reading puzzles me now. The Baltimore of my early childhood was, in retrospect, surprisingly white; the Vermont of my later childhood almost entirely so. And this was absolutely reflected in my reading.

In her own brief memoir of rereading, Dionne Brand discusses 'the complicated ways of reading and interpretation that are necessary under conditions of coloniality'. Reading the Western canon as a child, she suggests, is to encounter repeatedly a 'we' that is based on the exclusion of others; she describes searching not for inclusion, but simply to be addressed. Unlike Brand, I read and write from a majority position; the texts I describe were written for, and often about, readers like me. And yet even as a child, and more especially now, I recoil from the assumptions I find throughout these works, their implicit ideas concerning race, gender, class, and sexuality. I want to insist that these aspects were not formative, although of course they were. I want to make excuses for their authors. I want to distance myself. I want to pick and choose which elements I return to, and which I discard; I do not like the complications of this literary legacy. And this might be why, looking at these texts now, I'm drawn to the ones that centre on animals, as they feel like me and not like me.

Certainly I wasn't to find myself in a novel until several years later, when I read *Jane Eyre* for the first time. The class was divided, in a way I hope would not be sanctioned now, by gender, and all the boys were assigned Robert Cormier's *The Chocolate War* and the girls got to read Brontë, and I opted for the latter. And there is still no scene in all of literature where I see myself as clearly as in the opening pages of *Jane Eyre*, as she sits in the windowseat, reading about birds. I never much cared about Rochester or Bertha or all the grand romance of the central narrative. I just liked the story of a lonely child who found solace in reading, and very much wanted Jane and Helen Burns to find a lasting love. The world of boys' stories, as much as I read them voraciously, was almost a form of anthropological study, and this was, perhaps, easier when men were framed as animals.

And this was clearly the case with my own local celebrity, Rudyard Kipling. While Kipling is thought of as a writer of England and India, the great champion of the colonial project, he lived for some time just down my street, in a house called Naulakha, which he designed in 1892. The house was built to look like an overturned boat, although I've never really seen it as such. The house is now owned by the National Trust, and you can visit his study, and in that study you can find a fireplace, which was rebuilt by my father. I did not slake the quicklime mortar for that house, although I did for several other historical construction projects my father worked on around the same time. Kipling was, for me, a local writer, and it was in this house that he wrote *The Jungle Books*, among other texts. He lived there for five years, until a fight with his family across the street, in what was and still is called the Red House. If Grahame's world paralleled my own but was also removed, Kipling's world, or at least the world of his writing, was visible any day I wanted to see it.

Kipling did not think highly of my little town. He writes simply, in his peculiar autobiography *Something of Myself*, 'What might have become characters, powers and attributes perverted themselves in that desolation as cankered trees throw out branches akimbo, and strange faiths and cruelties, born of solitude to the edge of insanity, flourished like lichen on sick bark.' I still don't know if I agree with this description, although it amuses me. But the world he created in that house, a world of freedom and law – the Law of the Jungle – a world of cruelty and unexpected sympathy, still seems familiar.

Kipling's work, for the following generation, was something of a litmus test, a ground for political awakening. T. S. Eliot, W. H. Auden, and George Orwell all write of their childhood love for Kipling and their growing realisation that in his work there is something alien, troubling, distasteful. C. S. Lewis details how on reopening a work of Kipling's he is initially enchanted, and then soon finds himself 'sick, sick to death of the whole Kipling world', which he describes as 'unendurable – a heavy, glaring, suffocating monstrosity'. Readers who have not looked at *The Jungle Books* since childhood might find that their memory is founded at least as much on the Disney animation, and that there is much there to trouble them. It is not simply that, like *The Wind in the Willows*, the central story is scattered among other fragments, that there are poems and stories in which Mowgli does not feature at all, and are set as far away from India as the Bering Sea. It is that the entire tale is infused with ideas of death and power. There are few stories in the collection as striking as 'Red Dog', which depicts Mowgli's rise to power, the pleasantest part of his life, Kipling writes, because 'all the Jungle was afraid of him'. The story depicts what can only be described as a genocide, where many of the heroic wolves, and all of the villainous red dogs, or dholes, are slaughtered. Whether or not this was intended as a metaphor for colonial rule, the cruelty is astonishing. Much like reading *Babar*, I am alarmed to find that the stories I took to be straightforward tales of education are predicated on the destruction of others; I wonder, even now, how seeing my life in relation to these tales makes me complicit.

Just as he admired Grahame, Theodore Roosevelt enjoyed Kipling's animal stories, which he approached as moral fables, perhaps supporting his own ideas of dominance. It might seem peculiar that a president, even one known for his interest in – and destruction of – the natural world, would comment on such texts, and yet both the texts and the president were caught up in a larger discussion of what it meant to write stories about animals at all. After Kipling's success, animal stories proliferated. Ernest Thompson Seton's *Wild Animals I Have Known* was a staple of my childhood reading, alongside his adventure story *Two Little Savages* and his Boy Scouts handbook, from which I taught myself, unsuccessfully, to tie knots. Seton introduces his work with a note about the nature of animal stories: 'The fact that these stories are true is the reason why all are tragic. The life of a wild animal *always has a tragic end*.' The 1970s edition I have now, from the New Canadian Library, makes the same point on its cover, emphasising the scientific realism of the writing. Certainly as a child I believed these stories, and I believed their tragedy.

Seton, along with William J. Long, was one of a group now called the 'nature fakers'; as much as they claim to shy away from anthropomorphism, they present nonhuman animals as moral guides for humans. Some of their stories are famously preposterous: as much as they claim all of their work is based on close observation, stories of, say, a fox riding a sheep are so unusual that they attracted widespread scorn, not least from Roosevelt. As Ralph H. Lutts argues, Seton and Long emerged at a moment when Americans were forced to reconsider the relation between humanity and nature, a conversation that continues to this day. Seton and Long, he writes, argue that nature is fundamentally moral, and 'it is to nature that we must look for ethical guidance'.

These debates are not as clear in Kipling and Grahame, but form the context for their texts' reception. There must be something in their animal stories we can learn, some way of applying these lessons to ourselves. *The Wind in the Willows*, for an American child, must be one of the most escapist texts available, and yet we need to think about what escape might mean, and how we are still situated in the world.

Kipling and Grahame both present worlds in which the barriers between human and nonhuman are blurred. And they are worlds of travel, of opportunity. But the constant yearning in *The Wind in the Willows* is replaced in *The Jungle Books* with constant threat. Grahame's weasels and stoats are disruptive, to be sure, but easily defeated; Kipling's dholes are far more vicious. Kipling's stories end in death, in woe, while Grahame's end in triumph. And yet the two authors, whom I encountered at the same time, strike me as fundamentally similar. Both write out of their own unhappiness, whether in terms of Grahame's longing for the company of men or Kipling's own legacy of abuse, and his quite miserable childhood. Both see in the construction of order, of what they might call civilisation, a way forward. But civilisation, they find, is a fragile thing.

And this was, for better or worse, my own world. I don't remember much of my schooling from this time. I remember very few friends. Indeed, when we moved to Vermont neighbours observed, with no little concern, that if I were playing in the yard and a car drove by I would hide behind the nearest tree, afraid of abduction, of threat, of the unfamiliar. My mother was still mobile, and I remember brief hikes up a local hill, walks and picnics in local graveyards, and yet almost all of my memories of her are set indoors, just the two of us, talking at the kitchen table my father had made years before from the remnants of a bridge. I did not know, then, why she might be afraid, and I am wary of rereading her actions in too definitive a way. But already, having achieved to some degree the life she had imagined for herself, she was beginning to draw in, to restrict her world, to privilege the familiar over the new.

At the end of 'Wayfarers All', after Rat has listened to the stories of the seafaring rat, he sinks into a deep depression. He cannot explain to Mole what he has heard, how much these tales of the outside world have appealed to him. Mole prescribes him some poetry, and at last Rat slowly begins to write, the beginnings, Grahame says, of his cure. And this was the age too when I began to write, mostly stories of animals. There was, most famously, 'The Nozel Story', about some small mole-like creatures who lived under the floorboards, a story I vividly remember writing while lying on the living room floor, and which my mother later typed up, although both documents have now vanished. There were several stories directly mimicking Deborah and James Howe's *Bunnicula*, the story of a vampire rabbit with which I was much enamoured. Like Rat, and like Grahame himself, I began to try to make a world in which I could feel comfortable. I do not know if my mother had that option.

But I also saw the world around me, all the other stories. On 21 December 1988, a week before my tenth birthday, I was on my way to a neighbour's house. My neighbours, a retired couple from New York who, in the absence of my own grandparents, did their best to fill that role for me, had been kind to me all year; volunteering for the local school library, they had noticed that I needed more of the world, or more books, or more life, and so I had been taken out of my spelling classes to read and discuss Walter Scott and T. H. White, tales of heroism and transformation, and of great loss. They showed me films, too; that night it was to be the 1937 adaptation of Rudyard Kipling's *Captains Courageous*, another product of his Vermont career. Just before we left the house, I heard the first reports on the radio about the bombing of Pan Am Flight 103, which exploded over Lockerbie, Scotland, killing 243 passengers, 16 crew, and 11 people on the ground. It was not the first time I was aware of such tragedy – the explosion of the *Challenger* spaceship two years earlier, watched, like so many other children saw it, live in the classroom, the knowledge of American military involvement around the world: these had had their effect. But the sorrow I felt that evening was insurmountable. I began to imagine not just every person who had died, but their families, their friends and loved ones, the grief they must be feeling. And I was inconsolable. The world had never seemed so cruel. My reading had prepared me for heroic defeat, but not for this. And my parents decided to honour their appointment, and we drove through the woods as night came in.

I sat in the back of the car, and I sobbed. I was filled with a knowledge of my own death, of other people's deaths, of the fragility of experience. And we drove past a small farm that I associated with Danny Dunn, the hero of a series of science fiction stories by Raymond Abrashkin and Jay Williams of which I was very fond (although looking back, Dunn's suburban home is nothing like the house I placed him in). And we drove through a small, dark, wooded area that I always called Mirkwood. The stories of Kipling and Tolkien and a dozen other writers swirled around me, and became part of my map of the world. And it was almost enough. I knew that these houses and fields and woods could produce great miracles, that they were spaces where enemies could be vanquished, where discoveries could be made. And yet I knew, too, that just that day almost three hundred people had lost the map of their universe. That a town I had never heard of would be defined by a tragedy that was visited on them by surprise. And at some point I must have stopped crying. At some point I must have accepted that this was the nature of the world I inhabited, and that the stories with which I was surrounded were a defence, a panacea. But I knew it was only a temporary solution.

All childhood is an imagined world. And in that imaginative act, in the creation of our own childhood, we find ways to see our story in relation to others. We find a river, and we pronounce it Grahame's River Bank. We learn rules of behaviour, and we know that they are really Kipling's Law of the Jungle. And we make our own worlds, too, worlds in which we are less afraid, worlds in which we understand what's going on around us. And still, sometimes, we are alone, and still the world, sometimes, beats down on us, and our imagination cannot save us any more.

The Magician's Nephew

That the world had beat down on my mother I knew from the condition of her boxed set of C. S. Lewis's *Chronicles of Narnia*, along with that of *The Lord of the Rings*, which had been purchased sometime in the late 1960s. I asked once, reading them, why the pages were so crinkled, the bindings so loose, and was told, briefly, that they had been damaged in the tornado, although I was not told when or where this was. Over the years I learned that the tornado was not the only disaster of the years before I was born, the first years of my parents' marriage. It is difficult to reconstruct the story of their courtship now, but this is what I know, or think I know.

In the summer of 1968, one year after the summer of love, my mother was sent to a Christian summer camp somewhere in the outskirts of Baltimore. Her family was not particularly religious at this point, and the choice seems strange. My father was also at this camp; his family was even less religious. My parents were thirteen and fourteen, and they fell immediately in love. I have, it only occurs to me now, never been told the story of how they met, or what they thought of each other, but I know that by the end of the summer they were utterly smitten. They became engaged three years later. This was not, to say the least, a decision of which either set of parents approved. One set of parents, I've heard, threatened to involve the police. And yet I do not entirely know, outside of a difference of perceived class, what the problem was, only that no one believed people so young could be so serious about their future.

My father was sent to high schools outside of the city, and lived on his own in a small shack near Camp David, famous for the peace accords. And he was angry. At some point he was thrown out of school when he was involved in a fight, having eaten a seventeen-year locust on a bet and not been paid. The worst bet I made in high school was simply to eat an entire grapefruit peel, and it really wasn't worth the few dollars I collected, and I understand the sense of injustice. When he graduated whatever high school he was attending at the time, he was shipped off to Iowa State University, to be as far away from my mother as possible. Many years later, talking to my grandmother, she spoke of how their decision to send him there was a sign of how seriously they took his desire to be a farmer, because Iowa State was, I'm told, known for its agriculture degrees. And yet my mother, certainly, saw it as a hostile act, one directed wholly against her.

In high school my mother found herself in a love of languages, mainly Russian and Spanish, and I know she wanted to study them further, preferably at Middlebury College, and I believe that her parents told her they would not support her studies if she did not end her relationship, and so she concluded her studies and went instead to Iowa, to live with my father. I do not know how far my mother's language learning continued; certainly she kept a few books in the house that she must have acquired at that time, but she never spoke either language to anyone else. It was a private study, an attempt to reach out to a larger world that remained distant. My mother loved learning, but she loved my father more.

And here their troubles began, or rather, the troubles of which I know more.

In their final years of high school, and the year when my father was in Iowa and my mother still in Baltimore, they had been unable to afford telephone calls, and they recorded long letters on cassette, which they posted. I don't know how long the tapes survived, although certainly they had disappeared long before I was born. I know that that year they were utterly miserable, that they made terrible decisions about their lives, that they were unable to hold on. And yet when my mother moved to Iowa, it must have been strange, after four years of waiting, to finally be together. My mother worked in a computer lab, one of the few jobs she ever had, handling those voluminous punch cards on which computers ran. My father continued his studies, to some extent, and completed an associate degree after two years; in later years, his academic pursuits were rarely mentioned.

I do not know that they had many friends. They married at eighteen and nineteen, a secular ceremony, with one witness, an Iranian student they lamented losing touch with, and worried about after the Revolution, and the three of them went out for pizza with the justice of the peace who acted as celebrant. For many years this formed my ideal of marriage, and when I turned nineteen and had not had such a life, I felt over-the-hill already. I do not know where they lived, I do not know if they went to church, I do not know what they did for fun. But they were together, and that, they hoped, was enough.

The following years were filled with abject poverty. Not the sort of poverty I grew up with, where I brought kidney-bean sandwiches to school – widely mocked by my classmates, but which I like to think of now as a sort of proto-hummus – but real poverty. My father worked on a farm in Missouri, and they ate roadkill and the squirrels he could kill with a slingshot. They stole vegetables from fields. My mother was, perhaps, unemployed at this point, my father serving, it seems, one of those apprenticeships or internships that allow employers to neglect to pay their workers properly. They never mention knowing another person, although perhaps there might have been other farm workers at this point; I am not even sure where in Missouri they lived, or why they lived there.

And at some point my mother's kidneys failed.

There are two stories I could tell here, and so I need to tell them both. And I do not feel these are my stories to tell, and yet I am the only one who can tell them.

In the first story my mother is somewhere in Iowa, or maybe Missouri. One day, when my father is away at work, she decides to eat a foxglove, whether as a conscious suicide attempt or simply out of hunger, I do not know. Foxgloves are beautiful, pink and purple and white flowers hanging like ranged bells. They are the source of digitalis, a medication that helps control heart rate. They are also called witch's glove, and known for their toxicity; while rarely fatal, digitalis can cause nausea, vomiting, diarrhea, seizures, and hallucinations. Van Gogh's yellow period, they say, may have been caused by an overdose.

Foxgloves are everywhere in Derek Jarman's writing, and in his garden. In *Modern Nature* he describes them in militaristic tones: 'no blushing violets these, and not in ones or twos but hundreds, proud regiments marching in the summer, with clash of cymbals and rolling drums'. He notes, immediately afterwards, that the first use of digitalis to cure heart disease was by one Dr Withering, in the eighteenth century; few older herbal manuals mention the flowers. Foxgloves hail the glorious summer, and yet there is withering; he calls them both elves' and dead man's fingers.

In this story my mother is, consciously or not, looking for a way out, and she finds it in a poisoned flower, like some sort of fairy tale princess. She wants to poison herself just enough to make a change; she wants to poison herself more than enough; she is simply very hungry. She knows exactly what she is doing; she doesn't know at all. At some point, too, there is a tornado, and my parents hitchhike back to Baltimore where she can receive medical care. It is a story defined by gaps, by unknown motives, but also by the possibility of intent.

Or perhaps everything happened earlier. In the second story my mother is a hippy, going by the nickname 'Healthy', and it is the spring before my father is sent to Iowa. She and a friend decide to cook some pokeweed, a poisonous plant, rather like asparagus, whose leaves can be made edible with multiple boilings. They eat the plant, and my mother drinks the toxic water in which it has been cooked. My father asks himself, in telling me this story, if she knew it would be harmful: 'I don't know', he answers his own question, 'it was not a happy time in general'. Both stories allow for intent, the possibility that this was wholly a self-destructive act, and both allow for this to have been nothing more than a stupid teenage accident. I don't know if my mother even knew the truth.

In this story she is sent to the hospital, covered with purpura, the tiny bruise-like spots that are often associated with meningitis and typhus, as well as platelet, coagulation, and vascular disorders. They are not associated with pokeweed poisoning. Foxglove is also called, it turns out, *Digitalis purpurea*, which is very close, but not the same at all. She is very sick.

I've since learned about psychogenic purpura, or Gardner-Diamond syndrome, which produces such symptoms, described in a recent article in the *Indian Journal of Psychiatry* as 'repeated crops of bizarre, tender, ill-defined ecchymotic lesions' that tend to affect 'psychologically disturbed adult women'. Another article in *The Primary Care Companion for CNS Disorders* notes that it is a result of 'severe stress and emotional trauma' that is usually found in adult women, but sometimes adolescents; this latter case study focuses on a fifteen-year-old girl. The syndrome is extremely rare.

The pokeweed and the purpura may be wholly unrelated; neither of them might have led to kidney failure. Or perhaps they're all part of the same underlying illness. Or perhaps the physical symptoms are a manifestation of psychological damage.

Before going to Iowa my father went to work on a ranch in Montana for a summer, a job organised for him by his family, and while he was there my mother went into the hospital again. My father, too, knows little about this story. But by 1974, in Missouri, it was clear that things were seriously wrong, and by 1975, in Baltimore, my mother's kidneys had begun to fail completely. Whatever the causes, whatever the reasons, this is where all the stories lead. There is a part of me that wishes so much to know the truth, to know why my mother became ill, and yet I know it doesn't matter in the end. My mother was ill, and she would remain so for the rest of her life. Whatever happened in those years was, directly or indirectly, what led to her death.

Telling this story, these stories, is no less an act of rereading than telling the stories of children's books. There's a comfort in returning to an often-told tale, a sense of nostalgia, even a sense of purpose; there's the fear that you can't go back, that you must reinterpret this story, that it might not have meant what you thought. Patricia Meyer Spacks ends her book on rereading with the declaration that we never read alone; we read along with the author, with our past selves, with the text's past readers. We read, she says, to make up for the gaps left by our families, to gratify the emotional needs that our relations, our friends, failed to fill. And we reread, she says, right at the end, because we realise that our books have never been about escape, that they've never been supplemental, but that they have always been part of the stories we tell ourselves about who we are. And so too with my mother's stories. I tell them in order to place myself in a larger world than I feel I have access to. I tell them because if you share this experience with me, if we know the same stories, it might make them more real, more vivid, longer-lasting. If you know my mother's stories, it might give her entry into a larger world than she found in life. I tell them because the telling itself is a panacea. The story of a loss comes to replace the loss itself. And I tell these stories because they also fail to explain, they fail to console, they fail to give me the answers I still desire.

There are common features to both of these stories: at some point my mother ate a poisonous plant. This may have been an act of self-harm, it may simply have been stupid. At some point, there was unexplained bruising, which may or may not have been related. At several points, she was hospitalised, and may have contracted a disease. And whatever happened, it broke her body irrevocably. If I don't know the story, I do know the outcome.

This need to go back, to explain, to find a cause is central to C. S. Lewis's *The Magician's Nephew*. The Bodley Head edition of the novel from 1971, published right at the time my mother might have been making a toxic pokeweed stew, includes a quote from Roger Lancelyn Green on the cover flap, arguing that Lewis never initially intended to write the novel, but embarked on quest to explain the origins of Narnia after the first books in the sequence were a success. As a result, I remain peculiarly angry about more recent publications of the series, which label it the first book, as it makes sense much more as a retroactive framing.

Many children, I suspect, identify themselves by which of the Narnia books is their favourite. A book report from first grade indicates that I liked *The Lion, the Witch, and the Wardrobe* best, although it has since grown too familiar. Later I liked the more straightforward adventures of *The Silver Chair* and *The Voyage of the Dawn Treader*; not only did I name a doll for Eustace, but on All Saint's Day one year when I was five or six, asked to dress as my favourite saint for school – Halloween being far too pagan – I chose Puddleglum. Narnia was a gift for the sort of child who mainly shopped in Christian bookstores; the allegorical elements secular readers reject were simply familiar, while the adventure was far more exciting than other religious texts. Indeed, while I was banned by my parents from reading stories of witches, an exception was made for Lewis; while I know few defenders of *The Last Battle*, I've always liked its vision of heaven.

The appeal of Narnia, perhaps, is that it's always just out of reach. When we first moved to Vermont, there was an attic in the house, and in that attic there was a wardrobe, or at least a cabinet, and I was so sure it would take me there. Even now, when I walk from my office into the nearby town, I take care to pass beneath a particular road sign held up by two posts that you can just squeeze between, hoping this time it will be the portal it is clearly meant to be. It is not that I have ever, I think, believed that Narnia is a real place, but rather that it is always around the corner all the same. This is probably the appeal of all portal narratives and yet, although Oz should have somehow, technically, been closer, since you can reach it from America, I never sensed any possibility of a visit. Narnia, though, seemed local, somehow, familiar enough to be reachable, given enough luck.

This familiarity is partly formal. As Francis Spufford comments in his own memoir of childhood reading, the Narnia stories are always intertextual; while Tolkien took pains to create a world, Lewis borrowed whatever he had to hand in a way, says Spufford, that appeals 'directly to immediate, sensuous belief'. *The Magician's*

Nephew opens with allusions to an explicitly literary past. The setting, the reader is told, is the same world in which Arthur Conan Doyle's Sherlock Holmes is investigating mysteries and E. Nesbit's Bastable children are looking for treasure; it is also, we're told in the same paragraph, a world in which sweets were far nicer than they are today. As readers we know Doyle and Nesbit, and we know what it is to be disappointed by a sweet, and there seems no reason to separate the two worlds. Lewis's world is believable precisely because it is situated in a familiar literary context.

Yet this comfort, for many modern readers, is itself a problem. Alison Waller, in *Rereading Childhood Books: A Poetics*, argues that the adult reader cannot find the same joy in revisiting Narnia that they find in other childhood books, but instead 'the potential to both betray and disenchant'. The stories themselves are built around a principle of nostalgic return that is often soured; indeed, in both *Prince Caspian* and *The Lion, the Witch, and the Wardrobe* itself children enter Narnia having been told it is a magical land, only to find it cruel, distorted, and somehow broken. Adult readers may disapprove of Lewis's literary borrowings or, even more, of the heavy-handedness of his Christian allegory. Like Lewis's own experience reading Kipling, there may be a feeling that as a child we missed something important, something uncomfortable, that we can no longer overlook. This is certainly the approach Anne Fadiman takes when she uses *The Horse and His Boy* to introduce a collection of essays on rereading by various authors. She describes reading the novel to her eight-year-old son; she is dismayed to find very real threads of misogyny and racism in the novel, while her son is frustrated that she needs to explain these, and cannot let him relax into the story. Fadiman uses the scene to argue that initial reading has velocity while rereading has critical depth, and certainly there is something to this. Rereading books we always find more than we first saw, and much of what we find may disappoint us. But I think there's also, beneath this moment, the realisation that we can't, actually, go back to Narnia, and that maybe Narnia was never what we thought it was. Fadiman ends her essay with a curious comparison between our childhood reading and our parents: we begin, she says, by idolising them, and then we learn the truth, but perhaps we love them all the same. Fadiman, in reading Lewis to her son, teaches herself how to enjoy the book again, how to persist in a love which has been challenged.

The Magician's Nephew is Lewis's most concrete attempt to face these problems head-on. To understand the world we live in now, we have to understand the world that came before, and it might not be easy. We have to understand that what we believed was innocent, or noble, or good, might have been born of corruption, and learn to love it all the same.

Digory and Polly, our child protagonists, are led into adventure simply because it is a cold, wet summer and they must explore indoors; it is the same set-up as *The Lion, the Witch, and the Wardrobe*, so that even at the beginning of things, we already have a model for the narrative in place. It has odd echoes, too, of that famously cold and wet summer of 1816, when Byron, the Shelleys, and Polidori are forced to make their own entertainment on the shores of Lake Geneva, and so *Frankenstein* is born. The children find, inevitably, magic rings that allow them to move between worlds. Digory understands that these rings must work according to the principles of fairy tales, but his Uncle Andrew diminishes his worries as 'Old wives' tales', and presses on, trying to find a scientific rationale. The children travel to the dead world of Charn, where they awaken, accidentally, a great Queen, or Witch, and everything goes wrong.

Charn, and the Wood Between the Worlds, where all worlds can be accessed by the means of pools, were always the most memorable locations in the novel for me. In each, there is an eerie silence, a sense of absence, yet Lewis is excellent at delineating the ambivalent absence of the Wood in comparison to the cruel absence of Charn. The Narnia books are filled with passages where the life that should be present is somehow stilled, most famously the creatures who have been transformed to stone by the White Witch in the first volume. The worst thing that can happen in Lewis's world is not active violence, which can be countered, but the cessation of possibility. The Wood is a magical place because it allows for infinite futures; Charn is a deadly place because it has no future at all.

The Queen makes all manner of havoc in London, and eventually all of our human characters find themselves on a world that is yet to be created. Aslan appears, and sings Narnia into being, each animal emerging from humps in the earth, somehow echoing Plato's account in *Protagoras*, but comic and beautiful. The land itself brings everything to life – an iron tree and a toffee tree. Creation works, Lewis suggests, with whatever is to hand, and it is comic and joyous and beautiful. And so Narnia has been created, and populated, and this should be our origin myth. This is certainly the part of the story I loved most as a child, where a cab-horse is given both wings and a name, where the first moment of laughter is given its own story, where the relations between different species are first codified, but all of the animals are portrayed in loving harmony. But there is a coda.

Aslan tells the creatures that there is evil in this world, in the form of the Witch – it is perhaps inevitable, or at least sadly familiar, that in Lewis's work it seems evil is always in the form of a woman – and so it must be combated, and he appoints a London cabby and his wife, who have been swept into the adventure, to rule. But Digory is given a different duty, an act of penitence, where he must journey far into the wild in search of an apple. The echoes of Genesis and the story of the Fall here are not, perhaps, overly subtle. His journey is not only a punishment, a form of redemption, for bringing evil into the world, but stems from his own emotional complexity. Aslan tells him that 'Grief is great. Only you and I in this land know that yet. Let us be good to one another.' Grief tests humans in a particular way, and requires its own narratives. Digory journeys to the tree, and is tempted by the Witch, who herself eats the apple, playing the Serpent to her own Eve. But there is more, for what she promises is not knowledge, or life, for Digory, but life for his mother. The apple, she tells him, is the only thing that could save his mother from death.

It seems remarkable that I forgot, until the moment of writing these passages, that the novel was about a boy's desire to save his sick mother. While she is absent from virtually all of the story, the moral arc is, simply, whether one should save one person or the entire world. The novel is, it appears, about how one lives with grief. Reading it now I find a prevailing sadness scattered throughout; Lewis's sense that everything that is born is known in its loss reverberates across the pages.

Digory brings his apple to Aslan, who confirms that to him that the apple would have saved his mother, ' "but not to your joy or hers. The day would have come when both you and she would have looked back and said she would have been better to die in that illness." ' Instead, Aslan himself gives an apple to Digory freely, and it revives his mother more completely, more honestly. The simple moral here against theft, against selfish desire, about learning to wait to accept gifts from divine lions rather than seeking them yourself, is clear. And yet it's puzzling. Digory's mother's recovery is reported only briefly; she is given two lines of dialogue before eating the apple, and none afterwards, although it is reported that she, like Aslan – like my mother – takes to singing. Indeed, the story of the apple itself, from whose seeds grow the tree from which the titular wardrobe of the first volume will later be made, is shown as more important. There is no narrative of recovery; while the final chapter is called 'The End of This Story and the Beginning of All the Others', the story of Digory and his mother is barely allowed to begin.

The unspoken question is not only what it takes to save another person, but what happens next. 'Whereof we cannot speak', writes Spufford in his discussion of Lewis, echoing a phrase from Ludwig Wittgenstein that I spent several years intending to have tattooed on my arm (because I was that kind of student), 'thereof we must write children's books'. The grief that underpins the story, the desire to save someone, and the inability for Lewis to imagine what would happen if you did, is extraordinarily present. Lewis's most famous autobiographical work, perhaps, is *A Grief Observed*; *The Magician's Novel* might fairly be called *An Invisible Solace*. And yet in both texts, Lewis attempts to dampen his own grief. The autobiographical work, published six years after *The Magician's Nephew*, is one of the most common books given to grieving spouses, at least in American Christian populations, on the principle, perhaps, that reading someone else's experiences can help the bereaved make sense of their own. If our story is shared by someone else, it means we can progress through it. And Lewis's anger and confusion are apparent throughout. Late in the book, however, he argues that 'passionate grief does not link us with the dead but cuts us off from them'; it reduces the person who is loved into an object. (I don't know if Lewis read Freud, but I would like to see his response.) Instead, we must think of the dead as still with us, a relationship that continues to move and evolve. But *The Magician's Nephew* provides neither passion nor movement. Digory's grief is understated throughout – it is telling that he is framed in the title as a nephew, not a son – and his ongoing relation with his mother, provided by magic, is just as understated. Lewis cannot, in this novel, detail either grief or hope completely.

In some ways, Digory's dilemma at the end of the novel might be the story of every child who loses a parent – and thus, in many ways, of every child. Each loss makes us wonder what we might have done differently, how we could have saved them. And it remains unimaginable, no matter how hard we try.

Lewis drew much of his inspiration, as he freely admitted, from the work of George MacDonald. And MacDonald, who lived for a time several hundred metres from the office where I am writing these words, trusted hopeful futures even less. At the end of *The Princess and Curdie*, the sequel to the more famous *The Princess and the Goblin*, the kingdom has been saved, the king and queen rule in peace and harmony, and the world is put right. Two volumes of adventure result in a happily-ever-after, as we'd expect. And in the final nine sentences of the novel, he undoes it all: a new king emerges, he is greedy, the kingdom is destroyed, and all the people die. It is, without doubt, the strangest ending in children's literature. And if Lewis is not that cruel to his reader, I think he shares something of MacDonald's failure to be able to imagine what continued happiness would be like. For both writers, even the most fantastic tale cannot end in a depicted peace; this would be to misrepresent the cruelty of the world. Both writers approach their work from the perspective that only an outside force can offer salvation, and that humans, above all, need to be saved. While I might reject this mindset now, it formed me, and as much as I might want to represent my mother's life in terms of happiness, it remains difficult for me. Like Lewis, when I attempt to write about her, I write about myself instead.

My mother's kidney transplant was, and was not, exceptional. Although kidney transplants were first attempted in the late nineteenth century, the first successful operation was in 1954, in Boston, conducted between two identical twins. In America around 18,000 people now receive a kidney transplant each year, 70 per cent receiving their kidneys from deceased donors. Over the whole of the 1980s, over 71,000 renal transplants were performed in America; by the end of 2017, 114,958 patients were waiting for a transplant, with a median wait of 3.6 years, while approximately 13 people die each day waiting for a transplant. A 1990 study looking back on transplants between 1974 and 1988 notes that 10-year patient survival rates ranged from 27 to 67 per cent, with an average post-transplant duration of 14.7 years.

These are not, in themselves, comforting numbers, but I find the existence of numbers comforting. Certainly it is striking, even now, that my mother survived for thirty years with a transplant. Towards the end of her life she would find herself surrounded by interns whenever she entered a teaching hospital, called to marvel at someone with a lifespan that would have been nearly unthinkable at the time she had her operation. And when her kidneys began to fail again, of course I offered my own. I would have gone to the ends of the earth to retrieve her healing apple. But she refused.

My mother's transplant, and her long survival, has to be thought of as a triumph, even a miracle. She was far luckier than many. And I wish, now, that when she was alive I had spent more days thinking 'this is another day she is alive' than 'this is another day she might die'. But for my mother transplantation was also the entry to another world, a world of frailty, of strangeness. The steroids that she took made her fat, weakened her bones, made her unrecognisable to herself. The frequent hospital visits made her visible, made her body public, in a way she hated. Part of the reason she avoided having her photograph taken was her deep-seated belief that her body was no longer hers; it was based on someone else's life, it was radically transfigured, and she was not in control of it. In an essay called 'The Intruder', adapted into a very peculiar film by Claire Denis, the French philosopher Jean-Luc Nancy writes about his own heart transplant, and how it introduces a fundamental strangeness: 'My heart became my stranger: strange precisely because it was inside.' The transplant, he says, makes him a stranger to himself. His body wishes to reject the organ, and yet, he says, the transplant makes the entire question of what 'his body' is unanswerable. The drugs he takes to retain the organ also change who he is. For Nancy, the strangeness of the transplant is that it makes it impossible to say 'I' with any surety; there are multiple versions of the self, of the body, and they are always at war.

In the same way, my mother's body is not mine to write about. These are not my stories to tell. I do not want to call my mother 'disabled', because she herself never used that word; it is hard to think of her in later years, her mobility significantly reduced, her pain near constant, and not provide that frame. I do not want to point to the changes in her body as a negative when they were so hard fought-for, when they were what allowed her life. I do not want to point to a past I never knew as true, as authentic; this is my mother's nostalgia, not mine. And yet my mother did grieve her own life, passionately. Her recovery was only part of a story, and not one she could always countenance. She became strange to herself.

Whatever happened to my mother in the early 1970s, whatever choice she made or accident befell her, it made her life into the pattern of a fairy tale. There was a poisoned plant. There was an untellable recovery. And there was a sense of loss, of a world which had been reshaped. Her body became a narrative she could not understand.

Watership Down

It is impossible to tell my mother's story without talking about her faith, about her immersion in and escape from Christian communities, about her passion and rage and her abiding love of God. But it is also difficult. Certainly I do not want you to dismiss her beliefs, but even more than that, the story itself is elusive, and the most important part of the story is the one for which I have the least evidence.

My parents were mostly, perhaps, Episcopalian. That was the denomination of their summer camp, the denomination in which they remarried when they decided, when I was about four, that they needed to marry in the eyes of God, not just the law; it was the church in which I was baptised and confirmed. My parents were also Catholic; it was church to which they converted after my baptism, and again after my confirmation. My mother was buried in a Catholic graveyard. And they were everything between; there were periods in which they identified with, or attended services of, the Mennonites and the Brethren and the Congregationalists and a dozen small evangelical sects the names of which I can't recall. We went to Quaker meetings and services with electric guitars and embarrassingly uplifting songs; we met in stone churches and neighbours' living rooms. Of all of my mother's choices, the choice of how to believe, as well as what to believe, was the one she approached with the greatest passion. Religion was not a matter of adhering to a tradition, it was an active, personal search, and it never stopped. My mother read more works of theology than, I suspect, many theologians. Her favoured poets were Herbert and Donne. She embraced new doctrines and rituals wherever she found them. She loved God with her whole heart, sincerely and without reservation, and she found God in books and songs, if not always the formal structures of a church. She would disappear from churches with astonishing speed: a line in a sermon she didn't like, an awkward conversation over coffee, a difference of interpretation of the Bible, and she would wash her hands of the entire denomination. More than anyone I've known, she believed in an absolute, definable truth, and wanted no one to stand in her way.

So it is peculiar, given the individuality of her approach to religion, that the most important religious environment of my childhood was founded entirely on principles of community. It is a cheap joke to tell people that I grew up in a cult, although that doesn't always stop me. But all the same, when *Baltimore* magazine profiled the Lamb of God Covenant Community, a branch of an organisation called Sword of the Spirit, which was based in Catonsville, Maryland between 1982 and 1991, it titled its article 'The Cult Next Door'. My parents and I were members of Lamb of God, or Loggies, as the community referred to themselves, for only a handful of years, and they left, or were pushed out, quite quickly.

Since Lamb of God folded before the advent of the internet, it is surprisingly difficult to find information on the community. I have looked for years, and have found a Facebook page for survivors, a few footnotes in studies of evangelical and charismatic communities of that time, a single academic article, and a set of files on Scribd, the internet document repository, including letters between members and the Archbishop, complaining of misconduct, as well as a scan of the *Baltimore* article, all uploaded by a former member of the community. And nothing else. The community, whole unto itself, has almost completely vanished.

The *Baltimore* magazine article, while it presents itself as objective, is keen to emphasise the cult-like aspects of the LOG. At its height in the late 1980s, the journalist writes, the community included over 250 families, who 'agreed to submit to the authority of a small cadre of leaders' governing every aspect of their lives, not least questions of marriage, relationships, and the appropriate roles for women. Members tithed 10 per cent of their income, wives were subservient to their husbands, single women were treated with some distrust, and their romances were usually arranged for them by the church leaders. The article uses the term 'husband-masters', and I can only imagine my mother's laughter at being told anyone was her master, but that, nevertheless, was the nature of the world she and my father had chosen to join. The community was located in a fifteen-block radius in a Baltimore suburb; unlike the rural religious communities of the nineteenth century, who would often found their own town – or in a number of cases, take over the buildings and land of a previous, failed communitarian experiment – it was integrated into the community. Many of our neighbours worked in Washington, DC for the government, often for the military, sometimes for the Internal Revenue Service. The community was led by a man named Dave Nodar, whom the article describes as 'a khaki-clad saint' or 'a Svengali in Rockports', depending on the reader's perspective. The community hosted a school, which I attended only for kindergarten before my parents removed me to an Episcopalian school not far away. In many ways, the suburban world we lived in was more modern, more familiar, than that of any other part of my childhood. It was a world of uniformity: mostly white, mostly middle-class, mostly single-income families with fathers working nine-to-five, mostly houses that looked pretty much the same. It was the world you have seen in a thousand television shows and movies, quintessentially American. And yet, like an inverse *Rosemary's Baby*, it was dedicated to Christ, to worship, to uniformity of thought as well as action.

The article stresses how, while it might be surprising that a suburban enclave could be thought of as a cult, the corruption and abuse of authority, the control over people's lives, the simple strangeness of intentional community bears all the hallmarks of such movements; even Nodar, when he is interviewed, mentions the more famous cult in Waco, Texas, if only to stress that Lamb of God, whatever its faults, was not that bad. And yet when I read about Waco or Jonestown, the litany of communitarian terror that fills American newspapers, I still weep. I know what it is to trust your leaders and be led astray. I know what it is to devote your life to a higher truth and find it incompatible with the world you live in. I know these people. I know their joy in community. I know how easily it sours.

I do not remember the leaders, except that sometimes they would sing songs at services. I do not remember the rules about women's roles, and I am quite confident my mother had no part in them. But I remember the occasions where we were invited to speak in tongues, and a moment, when I was perhaps six years old, where I let the Holy Spirit ripple through me, bringing out unfamiliar noises, and wondered if maybe, just maybe, I was making the whole thing up. I remember the overwhelming communal joy of those services, every voice, every body, engaged in one common project. I remember the delight in blood and violence in the Easter play, the figure of the crucified Christ smeared with ketchup. I remember the tension over the need to belong, to make appearances at the right Bible study, the right prayer breakfast. And I remember, too, the loss of community, the way that, unlike our previous house in Baltimore, people didn't sit on their stoops and listen to ballgames together. I remember belief, and I remember the rigidity with which it was enforced, the joy of shared experience and the fear of being left outside of it.

Lamb of God was an example of what is called in the academic literature an NRM, or new religious movement, to avoid the derogatory implications of the word 'cult', and yet, as Judith Church Tydings argues in a lengthy 1999 article in the *Cultic Studies Journal*, even Catholic bishops charged with overseeing such communities often termed them cults. One interview subject Tydings cites says, in relation to Word of God, another branch of the same group of community as Lamb of God, that 'what began as a community focused on joyous, loosely structured prayer gatherings, evolved into a highly structured, religiously militant community with its own prescriptive culture and authoritarian control of members. Some charge that the community came to resemble a cult.' Another interview subject, a woman from Lamb of God itself, describes wearing trousers to take out the trash, both of which were not deemed appropriate for women, and feeling a sense of guilt and being watched. Both communities forbid men from household chores, and forbid women from taking the lead in conversation, or denying their husbands sex.

My mother wore jeans. She did not submit. And we raised rabbits.

I cannot overstate the importance of Richard Adams's *Watership Down* in my conception of the world. When the novel first came out my mother was in hospital, and the medication she was on, or the illness she had at the time, was causing her to go blind, and she described trying to read the final pages of the novel as quickly as she could, because if she never regained her sight, she needed to know what would happen next. She told this story often, although she never clarified the surrounding context: what mattered was not what was happening to her body, but her love of the story. When she was pregnant with me, she and my father saw the animated adaptation, and always told me it was my first film.

And, of course, it is a novel not just about rabbits, but about communities. Although we left Lamb of God in 1986, under severe disapproval, what I know of it comes from Adams's rabbits, who remain the best examples, to my mind, of the late-twentieth-century move towards intentional communities, and the problems that arise.

The first thing you notice, on rereading *Watership Down*, is how literary it is. While Lewis makes both explicit and implicit references to other works, Adams's use of chapter epigraphs positions the novel in a cultural context not often associated with children's animal stories. The opening chapters, for instance, begin with quotations from Aeschylus, Henry Vaughan, Xenophon, Shakespeare, Yeats, Napoleon Bonaparte (in French!) and the Bible, as well as the frequently cited R.M. Lockley non-fiction text *The Private Life of Rabbits*, upon which Adams draws throughout the novel. Like Walter Scott's use of epigraphs in his historical novels, these quotations often highlight the central theme of the chapter to come; the first epigraph, from Aeschylus's *Agamemnon*, describes a house that 'reeks of death and dripping blood', anticipating Fiver's prophecy of the danger coming to the warren. The epigraphs, like the explanatory footnotes peppered throughout – the first one, explaining Fiver's name, is on rabbit mathematics – indicate the seriousness with which the reader should take this story. This is not fanciful, Adams implies; we must take these characters seriously as rabbits, but we must also accept that their story matters as much as a human one, and that the rabbits' grief and terror is as real, and as worthy of recording, as our own. This rabbit world may not be ours, and yet we do, in a sense, know it already, because we know these surrounding stories. These are not the rabbits of Beatrix Potter, in their natty waistcoats. They are not, in a sense, reader surrogates, like Grahame's animals. And yet they are enmeshed in a world of text and sensory experience that is much like our own.

But the quotations do something else just as important: they create a community. When I first read *Watership Down* I doubt I knew who Aeschylus was, although I'd read some Shakespeare, and certainly plenty of the Bible. But in these collected voices, some familiar and some strange, I could begin to place myself. Adams makes us remember that we are readers, and that we never read a text without a surrounding context. We are participating in this story. And Adams wants us to take it to heart. We are given pronunciation guides; the first time the rabbits mention the mythical rabbit hero El-ahrairah, the Prince with a Thousand Enemies, a footnote tells us that the stresses are the same as the English phrase 'Never Say Die', and so the definition and the pronunciation become the same. And because of this generous impulse, we begin to incorporate the novel's language into our own. The term 'hrududu', plural 'hrududil', for motorcar, is not given a gloss, but that hasn't stopped me from using in to describe automobiles pretty much every day of my life, if only in my head, just as whenever I see rabbits feeding beside train tracks or a running path I think they are out for silflay.

I look for rabbits every day. Train journeys are the best, and I know where all the warrens are on the main East Coast line in Scotland. But in woods and fields, I scan every verge, every place where the grass might seem a little shorter, to see if there are rabbits there. And every time I find them, my heart leaps up, as if I have come home.

Watership Down in some senses follows an epic model, not unlike *The Odyssey*, but is unusual in having no clear hero. Fiver, the nervous, prophetic rabbit whose visions of the future underpin the action, was always my favourite as a child, and it's difficult not to see some of my mother's own life reflected here as well. Fiver is both outcast and leader; his visions are sometimes doubted and ridiculed,

and sometimes they make him ostracised, and yet the entire community must respond to them. But each of the rabbits contributes
to the group in their own way, and in narrative terms none is
favoured. This is not the story of Bigwig or Hazel or Blackberry or
Silver, although they all have their heroic moments, their own great
stories: it is the story of how they work together. The novel presents
the search for community as a communal endeavour; what the
rabbits need is to find a home that suits all of them equally.

There are many forms of community presented in the novel. As
they journey from their home the rabbits encounter communities of servitude at a farm, and artistic expression in the form of
a warren based, it seems, around an appreciation for avant-garde
poetry. (Go back and take another look if you don't believe me.)
Their own brotherhood – for like Grahame's animals, our initial
community is made only of males, although here it is at least significant to the narrative – is founded on the repetition of stories.
(Adams uses Grahame for one of his epigraphs midway through
the novel, in order to introduce an important river.) Listening to
the myths of El-ahrairah, they learn who they are, and what they
have in common. Adams, citing Lockley not in an epigraph but
in the body of the text itself, insists that rabbits 'are like human
beings in many ways. One of these is certainly their staunch ability
to withstand disaster and to let the stream of their life carry them
along, past reaches of terror and loss.' Their survival hinges, he
continues, on 'a blessedly circumscribed imagination and an
intuitive feeling that Life is Now.' Yet the chapter that follows this
declaration, titled 'The Story of the Trial of El-ahrairah', shows how
it is the rabbits' imagination and sense of the past that underpins
their existence. Bluebell tells a particular mythic story in response
to Dandelion's stories of the present, and that act of interrelation
is what gives the rabbits hope for the future. Likewise, it gives the
reader, or at least the reader who is like me, a way of integrating
multiple stories into their own sense of the present; the song of the

hedgehog Yona in this story – 'O Slug-a-Moon, O Slug-a-Moon, / O grant thy faithful hedgehog's boon!' – is rarely far from my mind. It is not a circumscribed imagination, nor a fidelity to the present moment, that ensures survival, but the ability to connect fable and experience through acts of communal storytelling that matters.

And this sense of the present and the past, the imagined and the experienced, blending together is what Efrafa lacks. Efrafa, the large warren governed by General Woundwort, has been the source of children's nightmares for the entirety of my life. Just flashing a still from the animated film on a PowerPoint in a lecture or talk tends to invoke a few shudders or whimpers, even now. The film especially – which, considering it takes 90 minutes to tell a story that takes Adams around 500 pages, is surprisingly faithful – is often considered scarring, violent, alarming, unsuitable for children. I've never thought it was anything but realistic.

Efrafa is how I understand Lamb of God, and all such communities. The imagined story and the lived experience are inseparable; neither is more true than the others. Efrafa is governed by the Council, and each rabbit in the Council has a particular duty: feeding, breeding, hiding. The rabbits are marked at birth and assigned to Marks based on their scar, and can only feed at prescribed times. The story of the woman who was ashamed for taking her trash out in public cited by Tydings seems very familiar here.

The *Baltimore* article highlights a similar chain of command in Lamb of God. Music services were designed to 'work the crowd into a shouting, fist-pumping fervor' and then calm them back down, bringing forth the moments of speaking in tongues that I, too, participated in, and prophecies from members of the community which, I learn only now, were not divinely inspired, but pre-approved. At single-sex prayer meetings members were encouraged to discuss their marital struggles, which would then be shared throughout the entirely male power structure, who would then send representatives to the couple in question, providing specific counselling and advice. Both love and God, and love of God, were controlled and directed.

The rabbits in Efrafa speak often of how Woundwort has broken their spirit; they have learned there is little point in resistance. But they, like the members of Lamb of God, and almost every similar community, also recognise the appeal of such structures. The outside world is filled with foxes, or the devil. The structures are in place to ensure that no harm befalls the members of the community; the leaders have seen how terrible the world is, and only they can keep you safe. An activist for the Cult Awareness Network named Doris Quelet, herself a devout Catholic, expresses her puzzlement that such a mundane cult could exist, that it bears comparison with Jonestown or Waco. There was no death, there was no stockpiling of weapons. But what they share is a fear of the world. Ex-members, says Quelet in the *Baltimore* article, 'have difficulty readjusting to society. They look at the world as an evil place and influenced by Satan.'

In *Watership Down* escape from the community is made possible by a variety of forms of external agency. There is a helpful seagull, and unwittingly helpful dogs. There is a boat and a train. There is, most curiously, a human intervention. Chapter 48 of 50 is called 'Dea Ex Machina', and inserts the reader immediately, surprisingly, into a human world, and the story of a girl named Lucy. Lucy's cat, Tab, finds an injured rabbit, and the language of description mimics human speech: ''Tweren't no rat, though; 'twas rabbit, layin' on its side by the kennel. It looked proper bad. Kickin' out an' all.' Human speech sounds strange; it is marked on the page as different. We are thrust into the human world, and it is uncomfortable. This is not simply an injured rabbit, we want to protest, it is Hazel, and he is noble and good and sorely wounded. And the human characters do not know this. But they save him, all the same. And they save him in the terms of a story: Doctor Adams says, as they release the rabbit, ' "But he could perfectly well live for years, as far as that goes. Born and bred in a briar patch, Brer Fox." ' Lucy and Doctor Adams do not know the story of *Watership Down*, but they know Joel Chandler Harris's Uncle Remus stories, featuring Brer (or Br'er, more properly) Rabbit, a trickster figure from African American oral traditions repackaged by a white journalist in the late nineteenth century. To save one rabbit is to save them all; to tell one rabbit story is to tell them all.

In this brief human interlude, Adams gestures towards not only the importance of storytelling in creating a community, but allowing movement between communities. The close interrelation of rabbit and human is apparent in Lockley's nonfiction work as well; like Adams, Lockley employs epigraphs – Keats, De La Mare, Chaucer, the Bible – to introduce his observations, from which he concludes that 'Rabbits are so human. Or is it the other way round – humans are so rabbit?' Lockley is aware of the dangers of overemphasising the animals' human attributes, and at the same time is unable to avoid giving many of the rabbits he observes human names as he observes them over many months. My favourite, inevitably, is Timid Timothy, the lonesome bachelor who is almost always described as skulking. Lockley's work is based on 1300 hours of observation from a tree-hide in a decayed elm; his assertions of the truth of his experiences echo Ernest Thompson Seton's work. *The Private Life of the Rabbit* and *Watership Down* are in many ways astonishingly close; not just the stories and behaviours, but even some of the description of local flowers and trees are common to both the novel and the earlier work of natural history.

Finding these connections, within and between texts, is the closest I can come to my mother's desire for life in community, her desire for an ordering principle or a common goal. *Watership Down* gives the reader a world so complete in itself that in its ending is its beginning. On the final page, Hazel dies, or rather, he is joined by a companion whose name he cannot remember, but whose ears shine faintly. This companion asks Hazel to join him, and they travel together, 'running easily down through the wood, where the first primroses were beginning to bloom'. And if the reader is like me, this is where they must set the book aside and have a good sob, but they might also remember that the novel's very first sentence was about the end of the primrose season. Hazel leaves the community, but the community continues on, and it is better because he was a part of it. All of the adventures the reader has witnessed are not only tied to a particular end, a better home for the rabbits, but are also part of a continual cycle in which all of the characters we loved and feared were only playing brief roles. And at the same time, Adams gestures towards an outside world: the epilogue begins with an explicit address to the reader who wants to know how the story ends. The story of this community carries over into our own, and if the rabbits go on living, so do we.

The same principle can be found, curiously enough, in John Humphrey Noyes's *History of American Socialisms*, from 1870. Noyes begins his mammoth survey of intentional communities with the work of another scholar, an A. J. MacDonald who died of cholera in New York in 1854, and adds to it. The book itself is largely a collection of documents – letters, anecdotes, testimonies – about a wide variety of communities, from the famous Brook Farm and New Harmony to much more obscure groupings that lasted only a year or two. Noyes is interested in the underlying philosophies of these communities, but also their economic viability: the cost of the land, the cost of food, the income the community received are just as important as the question of why they incorporated in the first place. His own effusive commentary then attempts to summarise what made these communities work, and why they failed. He ends his chapter on the Trumbull Phalanx, an Ohio community originated by socialist enthusiasts in Pittsburgh, Pennsylvania, that lasted from the spring of 1844 to the end of 1847, with a striking eulogy.

What a story of passion and suffering can be traced in this broken material! Study it. Think of the great hope at the beginning; the heroism of the long struggle; the bitterness at the end. This human group was made up of husbands and wives, parents and children, brothers and sisters, friends and lovers, and had two hundred hearts, longing for blessedness. Plodding on their weary march of life, Association rises before them like the *mirage* of the desert. They see in the vague distance, magnificent palaces, green fields, golden harvests, sparkling fountains, abundance of rest and romance; in one word, HOME – which is also HEAVEN... Instead of reaching palaces, they find themselves huddled together in loose sheds – thirty-five families trying to live in dwellings built for one. They left the world to escape from want and care and temptation; and behold, these hungry wolves follow them in fiercer packs than ever... This is not comedy, but the direst tragedy. God forbid that we should ridicule it, or think of it with any feeling but the saddest sympathy.

All people, Noyes suggests, share the same utopian vision, a vision of association, or socialism in the broad sense – not tied to creed or political theory, but the importance of the social itself. And these dreams fail. The communities are corrupted. Leaders seize too much power, or do not assert enough. The dream of a self-supporting community fails when it turns out that its members do not know how to grow the right crops. Living in close conditions, people squabble, and those petty disagreements become unsolvable problems. And this, says Noyes, is tragic. We should pity these failed communities, because they went further than most of us in trying to achieve a basic human goal.

Certainly it was a common goal in the America where I was born. Benjamin Zablocki's *Alienation and Charisma: A Study of Contemporary American Communes* was published in 1980 as, says Zablocki, the vogue for intentional communities was already fading. The communities he studies – some large and some small, some urban and some rural, some secular and some religious – flourished, if that's the right word, between 1965 and 1975, at which point people lost interest. Rural communities began to decline in 1971, and urban ones in 1976 and yet, in 1980, just as my own community was coming into being, he looks at this trend as a particular moment in American history, one that echoes the nineteenth-century phenomenon Noyes describes, and yet which is also already over.

And yet Zablocki begins the book with the simple assertion that the problems that face these communities, the questions of how to live together, and how to reach a common decision, are those that face all people (and all sociologists). Intentional communities are not a microcosm of society, but if we cannot understand why likeminded people find it so hard to live together, we have no hope of understanding why people who might be more prone to disagreement have the same problems. Communities, he says, begin with the very simple feeling that the world is too large, and we must reduce it to a manageable size. Communities arise from a combination of alienation from the world and, often, the charisma of a particular leader giving rise, he says, 'to an infrastructure of hierarchy beneath a façade of egalitarianism'. The members of the communes he looks at were more likely to be white than not, they were more likely to come from stable homes than not, they were more likely to be middle-class than not, and yet there was some fundamental lack of love in the world that they believed a community could compensate for. And what they found, regardless of the structure or fundamental ideology of their own particular community, was communion. Communion, he writes, 'is experienced as a shared altered state of consciousness in which the problems of autonomy and inequality are temporarily solved. Community is felt as real. It is a solution to the problem that is modern life. And this is as true of the twentieth century as the nineteenth.

Zablocki's book is full of graphs and figures and detailed methodologies; it is a work of science. *History of American Socialisms*, similarly, rests on detailed testimonies, on facts as far as possible. But Noyes is far from an impartial observer, for the book ends with his description of the Oneida community, of which he was leader. All of the first-person recollections and the newspaper clippings about failed communities have shown him how to succeed. He lists the basic tenets of a successful community in a discussion of both his own community and Shaker communities, emphasising the importance of 'peculiar religious views'.

Religion as the basis, inspiration as the guide, Providence as the insurer, reverence for the Bible, Communism of property, unanimity in action, abstinence from proselytism, self-improvement instead of preaching and publicity, liberality of culture in science, art, literature, language, mechanics, philosophy, and whatever will help to give back man his lost mastership of the universe...

These are the principles of Noyes's own 'Bible Communism', which he had been pursuing for some decades already. Some of these principles are familiar from my own life, although Lamb of God would not have condoned anything like liberality of culture. In both texts, the desire for unanimity is paramount. Community works only if thought, as well as property, is communal.

But the peculiarity, as it were, of Noyes's religious views was soon to become well known. In his book, Noyes explains the importance of not keeping men and women in separate spheres, but in breaking down every boundary, so that all labor was equally shared, whether domestic or external. In practice, this also led to what Noyes termed 'complex marriage', which was indeed complex. To free his community from the exclusivity of traditional marriage, sexual relations between all members were encouraged, or at least heterosexual relations, provided that men exercise coitus reservatus, or male continence – intercourse without ejaculation. So long as no children ensued, all sex was welcome. Consent was explicitly encouraged, pairings were sanctioned by the authorities, and the fundamental rules were that relationships should not last long enough that the parties fell in love or produced children. Young men, whom Noyes believed could not control themselves, were taught sexual techniques by post-menopausal women. Noyes himself took the opportunity to introduce young women to sexual activity, a sort of jus primae noctis, or right of the first night, that was exercised not long after the onset of puberty.

So yeah, that's gross. Noyes's mission to show the possibility of freedom from ideas of original sin, to show that human communities could be signs of God's benevolence, was built on what can only be considered prolonged sexual abuse. I find reading about the Oneida community as heartbreaking as reading about Jonestown, because I know these people, I know their innocence and their will to believe, their instinctive trust in their leaders, their belief that in every way they were doing the Lord's will. I know their petty jealousies and their secret reservations. I know their fury at betrayal, and their simultaneous desire to keep the flaws of their community hidden from the wider public, to insist that despite everything, despite everything, what they had attempted was simply to do, and to be, good.

And Noyes matters because he was my neighbour.

I wasn't party to the conversations that led my parents to leave Lamb of God. Some years later, attending an academic conference in the Midlands, I was able to visit one of their friends at the time, who herself had fallen in love with an Englishman over their shared appreciation of C. S. Lewis, and left the community around the same time as my parents. I was astonished to hear her fond memories of her time in Baltimore, her delight in talking about what she consistently called 'The Community'. My parents were, she acknowledged, never wholly welcomed in it, never really a part. She insisted on a vibrant community that she had been sorry to leave, and yet understood that for my parents there had been no other choice.

However it was that my parents left Lamb of God, they looked around for like-minded communities wherever they might find them, and eventually found a Brethren congregation in Putney, Vermont which happened, over a century earlier, to be the first location of Noyes's communitarian experiments.

Noyes was born in Brattleboro, the son of a former minister turned shop clerk, and a fairly close relation of President Rutherford B. Hayes. He attended Dartmouth College, in whose hospital waiting rooms I spent large portions of my childhood, and when he was twenty, in 1831, he attended a revival meeting in neighbouring Putney, leading to what he called his second conversion. By 1840 he was publishing a newspaper, the *Perfectionist*, explaining his theological beliefs, and had likewise founded a community, the Putney Corporation, or Putney Community – initially called the Putney Bible Class, or Putney Bible School, and then the Society of Inquiry, and the rather official 'Contract of Partnership' – dedicated to enacting these same theological ideals. Although he stressed the informality of the community structure, and the extent to which all followers were guided by God, he also established a set of written instructions through which to control his followers, and presented himself as final arbiter of moral behaviour. He likewise instituted his first attempt at complex marriage in Putney, having fallen in love with a woman named Mary Cragin while already married. The community abided by these new rules for over a year until 1847, when Noyes, in offering counsel to a potential new member, explained his sexual philosophy, and was almost immediately reported to the state's attorney. Noyes and his followers fled to Oneida, New York, where their new community was founded.

The pattern happens again and again. A charismatic man is inspired by God to create a new order, a new vision of heaven on earth. He finds followers, and he creates a structure by which this new heaven must be ordered. And whether the structure emphasises chastity or sexual freedom, it seems that the community must always be founded on the control of women's bodies. The social rules of Lamb of God, the complex marriage of Putney and Oneida, the restricted breeding and mating regulations that Woundwort enforces in Efrafa – it is the same pattern, again and again. And it is crucial that these communities are not inherently evil. Spencer Klaw, in his history of the Oneida community, stresses that women were, in many respects, treated more as equal partners, intellectually and physically, than in the surrounding secular society. One interview subject in the *Baltimore* article says that Lamb of God 'elicits loyalty because we wanted to love God and one another'. The members of these communities are not fools or naïve, they are not simply duped by a man in search of power; they find, and find truly, a harmony, a way of existing in the world, that they have not found in the outside world.

Several of Noyes's children published autobiographies; his son Pierrepont's presents his life until the age of sixteen, coinciding with the height of the community and Noyes's departure, in exhaustive detail. It is 'a strange world' into which he was born, be begins, where he was separated from the rest of humanity. Although he writes of how odd the external world appeared to him, he repeatedly asserts that his own life was not more pious than that of any other child in the era. It was an ordinary childhood in many ways, unusual only in its sense of purpose and cohesion. He ends his introduction to the text asserting the solidity of this community: 'there was nothing tentative about that environment, either spiritual or physical. The framework of our religion seemed final, human relations fixed, and both buildings and businesses showed that the Community fathers planned with faith in their permanence.' This is, I think, the desire of every individual who enters into community: the assurance not only that you have found a way to be with others, to know yourself in relation to them, but that you have entered a world founded on the truth. Submitting to rules is a way not of diminishing the self, but demonstrating that you have found the right path through the world.

And yet we still recoil, perhaps, from these visions. At the end of *New World Utopias*, his pictorial history of twentieth-century American communities of all sorts, filled with photographs of abandoned buildings and deserted fields, Paul Kagan asks if there are 'ideas and a structure of community life through which we can see the fragments of ourselves as they really are, not as they should be.' He expresses frustration at the voice of disillusioned community members who had not realised how difficult it would be: 'He says he worked hard, but he had no idea it would be necessary to depend upon the outside world so much – even for sustenance. It is an interconnected world, we reply to ourselves. Didn't he know that?'

Of course we all know this. And yet the desire remains. Kagan's book was published in 1975, at the height of the self-sufficiency movement that also produced the *Whole Earth Catalogue*, from which much of my agricultural, social, and sexual education came. The dream of community is always tied to the realisation of its failure, and the two are ultimately impossible to separate. We want community precisely because we know, at some level, that it can't last. Community allows us to be the versions of ourselves we wish we were, the people who are kind and nurturing, who can always move past selfish desires to the greatest good. Every community, whatever its founding principles, is utopian.

Most of the communities Noyes discusses lasted for two or three years; the ones in Zablocki's and Kagan's books were similarly shortlived. And so too my mother's communities. We abandoned the Putney community we'd moved 400 miles to join within a year or two, rejoining the Episcopal Church (and leaving it, and rejoining, and endlessly on). My clearest memory of our time with the Brethren was not community, but being just outside it, attending a prayer breakfast and sitting beneath the table of a local restaurant, reading *Macbeth* of all things, surrounded by the hanging table-cloth. It was inevitable, perhaps, that I become Lockley's Timid Timothy, skulking around the corners of a more vibrant life.

But my mother never stopped searching for communities. Sometimes I think she would have been happier as a medieval anchorite, searching for God by herself. Certainly I hear my mother more clearly in Julian of Norwich than in works by people like Noyes. Julian writes, early in the shorter version of *Revelations of Divine Love*, that she 'wanted to live so as to have loved God better and for longer, in order that I might, through the grace of that living, have more knowledge and love of God in the bliss of heaven', and I cannot find any words that more aptly summarise my mother's faith. She did not always want to stay alive; she could not always see how it was even possible. But life was worthwhile, she believed, because she could, through living, grow in the love and knowledge of God. And this required community: it was only the presence of others that let her own love develop.

I cannot enter into those communities now. I have attended a handful of weddings and funerals in the past decade, a few Christmas carol services at the local cathedral, and for a moment I become part of that community again. I hear the people around me singing with one voice, and I join in, and we are the glory of the earth. And it crashes down around me. I become lost and afraid. I begin to cry. I have not sung a hymn without crying in many years. I feel that pull, that need to belong, and I feel pushed back out. In my work, in my life, I stumble upon moments where I feel I have entered this true community. I feel embraced; I feel honest. And then I am alone again, and still afraid. Testimony after testimony I read tells me the same thing: there is no loneliness like the loneliness of someone who had community and lost it.

But where I find community is in the nest of words and quotations, the parallels and echoes between texts. This, for me, is the one song, the unified voice, that my mother sought. And I find community in rabbits, in being part of a shared world. *Watership Down* provides a happier ending than that of any human community I know; after all their trials, the rabbits finally come home, and not just the original rabbits, but new members who have emerged from the various failed communities depicted over the course of the novel. Hazel himself, in death, enters into the community of myth and story. The communities of the living and the dead become blurred. The warren in Watership Down has become a place of welcome, of true communion, that is not limited by time or place.

It is this lack of limitation, or this idea of expansion, that might define community. The novelist Marilynne Robinson writes about the role of the fiction writer in explicitly Christian terms; she says that her conception of how fiction and community work comes from Jesus's actions, which she calls 'presence in absence'. Community, as she defines it, 'consists very largely of imaginative love for people we do not know or whom we know very slightly', and fiction is 'an exercise in the capacity for imaginative love'. We learn to love through stories. We build community by recognising not only the validity of our experienced world, but the world we do not see, but recognise is just as true as our own.

This is the community Adams envisions, in a sense. *Watership Down* is the story of some particular rabbits, but also the story of how they grow in their sense of self, in their love for the world, through storytelling. Storytelling is how you come to understand your own life in relation to all the lives that are lived around you. It is how you become more than yourself. And it is the story of how the reader enters this world too, learning to love imagined rabbits. And for me, it is a way to love my mother, to feel her presence in her absence.

This is not the community I grew up in. Lamb of God – like Oneida, like Jonestown, like any community that might spring to your mind, perhaps – was poisoned by a failure of imagination. In thrall to one person's stories, the members of the community were unable to hear others; transfixed by presence, they were unable to incorporate the absent. But in remembering that community, I begin to understand my mother's desire to insert herself into a particular story. My mother's constant movement might not simply reveal the limitations of her communities, but the way each community is a story, each story a community, and each of them gives us a new way to live.

The Secret Garden

My mother was abused.

Four words, a simple sentence, and it is one I have never spoken out loud, formed so directly. I do not know how I know that she was abused, or what sort of abuse took place. There is only one story I have heard. Sometime in their thirties my mother was speaking to her sister on the phone, and my aunt, so my mother reported, was complaining about some family cutlery she had received from my grandparents. There was a serving fork, and it was badly bent. 'Of course,' said my mother. 'That's where it stuck in the wall when my father tried to stab me with it.'

Around the same time my mother received a shipment of the family china from her parents. She opened the boxes to find that they had not included any packing material, and some of the plates were already broken. And she methodically picked up every plate, every saucer, and smashed it on the kitchen floor, screaming.

She was more likely to speak of the abuse her father suffered as a child. His mother hated him, as did his older sister. His older sister, family lore has it, was, in fact, his mother. But whatever the circumstances, it was an unhappy childhood. I do not know if he was beaten, but he was, when young, locked in a room that they filled with gas, trying to poison him. I do not know how he survived.

I do not know if the attempted stabbing was a single occurrence, or part of a larger pattern of physical violence. Everything I know about people leads me to believe the latter, but perhaps I am wrong. I do not know if my mother was sexually abused, but I know that she tried not to bring friends home, because she believed her father to be a danger. I last saw my mother's father when I was six, because I was now at an age where it was, she thought, unsafe to be around him. I do not know if these fears were justified, but I know that my mother lived so much of her life in fear.

And I know this through the body – not just hers, but mine.

I remember my kindergarten classroom more clearly than any other. There was a water table positioned to the left of the door – a deep-lipped table filled with water and all manner of floating toys, and one of the great joys of my childhood. There was an art corner further along, and a costume area opposite it. The costumes were placed beneath a set of stairs that led to a loft, and the loft was where the classroom library was. And of course all I wanted, as much as I loved the water table, was to climb the stairs, to remove myself from my classmates and enter the world of books. And I did not know, properly, how to climb stairs.

My mother was far more mobile at that point than she would be later, but clearly she must have struggled with stairs, and would move up them slowly, two feet on every step, leaning heavily on the railing. And I knew no differently. And the loft staircase had no railing, and I did not know how to climb it. There was no physical impediment; I simply could not move in any way other than my mother moved.

Later, my mother, her bones made fragile by prednisone, would develop an overwhelming fear of ice, and would shuffle her feet inch by inch, leaning heavily on a wooden walking stick my father had carved for her. Even now, to take a full step on the ice seems strange to me, terrifying.

And if this physical echo is true, what of all the others? Why is it that as an infant I could not bear to be naked, even to be changed? Why did I vomit when strangers touched me? Why do I flinch, even now, when someone puts their hand on my back?

My mother was alone in her body, and so I have learned how to be alone in mine.

Trauma, every theorist agrees, is the thing you cannot say, the story you cannot tell. It is something that is never fully experienced the first time, never fully incorporated into the story of your life, and yet which keeps reappearing. It is a rupture, it is a wound. And if my mother never spoke of trauma, it is because trauma is unspeakable.

In her account of Bechdel's *Fun Home* Meera Atkinson differentiates between post-traumatic stress disorder, which often arises from one particular traumatic experience, and complex post-traumatic stress disorder, which arises from chronic situations, such as long-term abuse. This latter category, she writes, is more likely to appear in what she calls 'familial transmissions'. What cannot be spoken by one generation becomes part of the following one. Complex or chronic trauma pervades every relationship, shapes every experience. This trauma is not abstract or disembodied, Atkinson writes, but bound up in grief, in shame, in melancholy and numbness. It is experienced through the body, and it is transmitted through the body.

The spring after my mother died I was exhausted, unable to stay awake for more than a few hours at a time. I finally managed to go to the doctor, and while they failed to diagnose either the glandular fever or depression that were clearly the cause, they were intrigued, horrified, by the discovery that I was a carrier of hepatitis B. I'd known this since I was eighteen, and went to give blood for the first time, and received a scathing letter from an official-sounding body informing me that I was never allowed to give blood again. My parents simply said they had always meant to tell me this might be a possibility, and just hadn't had a chance. And I knew I was marked, and I knew to be careful. But the doctors in Scotland were first outraged, and then curious. For they knew how hepatitis had been transmitted through the early dialysis machines, and they were excited, unnaturally so, to see a simple miscalculation have effects decades later.

My mother's period of dialysis left her with an arm blindingly white with scar tissue; my own disease is so very minor in comparison. And yet I know, in a more literal way than most, that it is her blood that flows in me. Her body is my body, her bones my bones, her fragility my fragility.

I do not want to say that I am traumatised. I do not want to overlay my own experience onto my mother's and so explain her, force my voice on top of hers, reduce her life to an explanation for my own. And yet there is no external truth I can appeal to, no witnesses, no documents; there is only the evidence of my own body. I know how to disappear in a crowd. I know how to find a door. I know how to run.

Judith Herman writes of the simultaneous hyper-arousal and disconnection experienced by victims of trauma. There is no baseline of attention; instead, their bodies are alert to danger. At the same time, she writes, traumatic events 'call into question basic human relationships. They breach the attachments of family, friendship, love and community. They shatter the construction of the self that is formed and sustained in relation to others. They undermine the belief systems that give meaning to human experience.' While the victims of a single traumatic experience may feel that they are not themselves, victims of chronic trauma may lose their sense of self entirely. Trauma, like pain, unmakes the self.

Was my mother's longing for community a response to trauma? Was her inability to stay in community based on an inability to relate as a self to others? Or was it simply a phenomenon of its day?

In their account of transgenerational trauma, Nicholas Abraham and Maria Torok go further. Symptoms, they argue, may not be based on what has happened in the victim's life, but on someone else's experiences. Abraham and Torok use the idea of the phantom, drawing on Shakespeare, to explain what they mean. The phantom is an invention of the living, to be sure: 'what haunts are not the dead, but the gaps left within us by the secrets of others'. A catastrophe has happened in one generation; its effects are felt by the next. It might seem fanciful to move from trauma to ghosts; the first time I read Abraham and Torok I simply rejected their notions. How, I insisted, could someone else's experience direct your own life, except as it was shared and spoken about? They compare the phantom to a ventriloquist and I, I want to insist, am no dummy.

And yet.

My mother's story is filled with gaps, this I know. And I am haunted by them. I do not know if the discourse of trauma is useful here, if it is true. I worry that I am treating my mother's life like a text, like something to be analysed, and that in doing so I am making her a case study, rather than a full, vibrant, person. I worry that I have confused causes and symptoms, that I have placed my emphasis on the wrong things. I worry that the more I try to speak to my mother's experience, the more I make her invisible. But still, these accounts feel true to me. In reading Atkinson and Abraham and Torok, in reading D. W. Winnicott and Melanie Klein, again and again I have the same reaction, where I dismiss so much of the work, I swear that it is irrelevant to my life, and then it hits, and I find a sentence so true I cannot breathe.

Alison Bechdel has a similar reaction. In *Are You My Mother?*, the sequel, of sorts, to *Fun Home*, she documents her struggle not only to understand her mother, but to write about her at all. The book is filled with quotations from Winnicott and Virginia Woolf, and she imagines them passing on a particular street, late in 1924 or early in 1925. She draws maps showing how they could have been on their way to separate appointments and happened across each other, unaware. Because if there is a pattern, if there is a connection, then there is an explanation. If Woolf and Winnicott live in the same world, then Bechdel and her mother can live in that world, and it can be explained. But it might, she knows, just be fancy.

The first time I lectured to a group of undergraduate students on Woolf I read the whole of the long passage from *Moments of Being* where Woolf says, of her mother – who died at forty-eight, one year younger than mine – that 'If what I have said of her has any meaning you will believe that her death was the greatest disaster that could happen.' I was sure, after the lecture, that my students had not seen me cry. I was wrong.

Woolf goes on:

it was as though on some brilliant day of spring the racing clouds of a sudden stood still, grew dark, and massed themselves; the wind flagged, and all creatures on the earth moaned or wandered seeking aimlessly. But what figures or variety of figures will do justice to the shapes which since then she has taken in countless lives? The dead, so people say, are forgotten, or they should rather say, that life has for the most part little significance to any of us. But now and again on more occasions than I can number, in bed at night, or in the street, or as I come into the room, there she is; beautiful, emphatic, with her familiar phrase and her laugh; closer than any of the living are, lighting our random lives as with a burning torch, infinitely noble and delightful to her children.

That moment of recognition is something I share. I might not want to say, or she might not want me to say, that she was infinitely noble, but surely her death caused all creatures on the earth to moan. And just as surely, she is there on the street, in the next room, just out of reach and always close.

I see my mother everywhere.

I see her when I tell my students about Shirley Jackson, a woman whose life was shaped, her biographers tell us, by the fact that her mother did not love her, a woman who lived, like mine, in a remote part of southern Vermont and made stories. When I read Jackson's novels and stories I hear my mother's voice, somehow. When I went to the cinema to see Josephine Decker's film *Shirley* – with a script by Sarah Gubbins, based on a novel by Susan Scarf Merrell – combining biographical elements of Jackson's life with elements from Jackson's novel *Hangsaman*, I evaluated Elizabeth Moss's performance in the lead by how well she seemed to mimic my mother. She did very well. It helps that *Hangsaman* is my favourite novel, and my favourite account of trauma. It helps that the film was shot, in part, on the Vassar College campus, and there are actors who sit in the Japanese maples in the quad, underneath which I once had a very long and serious conversation with a squirrel, when I was not well.

And yet I remain entranced by the way that Moss somehow manages to get my mother's chin exactly right.

And more, and everywhere. For years I worked in book retail, and once, standing by Hilary Mantel's side, I was so sure that she was my mother I gasped, and ran away. I see my mother in the supermarket, in the pages of my books, in a passing song.

And the moment passes, and she is gone again. Woolf said that when she finished *To the Lighthouse* her mother disappeared. She speaks of psychoanalysis, and says that her mother was laid to rest. But mine hovers on, still waiting.

The final image *Are You My Mother?* depicts Alison, as a child, and her mother, seen from overhead, a God's-eye view, surrounded by an enormous black border. Bechdel writes that 'There was a certain thing I did not get from my mother. There is a lack, a gap, a void.' But in its place, she says her mother 'has given me the way out.'

I do not know if my mother has given me a way out, but she has given me those gaps, that lack. My mother was 'good-enough', in Winnicott's phrase, in a way that her own mother was not, and yet I am still shaped by her parents, by the way that every interaction with me my mother had was a conscious attempt to undo their damage, to do something differently. For Winnicott, the role of the good-enough mother is to give back to the child his or her own self. Perhaps this is what my mother did; perhaps she simply gave me her own self, made new.

At the moment I am writing these words I have just read Katherine Angel's essay *Daddy Issues*, which combines Winnicott, Bechdel, and Woolf, and makes me feel I must, I must, be on to something. If Angel can find this connection, so can I. As Angel reads Bechdel's reading of Winnicott, the child needs an object it can destroy, and which can survive that destruction. She writes: 'Creating the capacity for love is the hardest thing a parent has to do, and it is hard for parents to do it if they need love from the child in order to feel themselves to be real.'

It was hard for my mother, certainly. My mother fought hard to have me, against the advice of her doctors. She fought hard to keep me safe, not only from her parents but from an oddly numerous list of men close to me – my godfather, my headmaster – who were later charged with abusing children. In later years she fought hard simply to keep me alive, to make sure that my own self-destructive tendencies were not part of a familial heritage. And she fought hard, at the same time, to be loved, to make herself real through me.

My mother made her own gaps material. If I had more pictures from my childhood I could show you how in any social gathering, where people were standing or sitting and talking, my mother was sitting on the floor, off to the corner. She would tell jokes, she would make herself a clown, and then she would become invisible. Her body, so long a source of interest to doctors, was both too present and not present enough. She would make herself the centre of attention so that she could disappear again. My mother made a space in the world as a way of navigating absence.

She was, simply, afraid of people. She was afraid of not being loved. She was jealous of my father, she was jealous of me; she was angry at a world that seemed so much easier to navigate for other people.

Jacqueline Rose makes the same connection between Winnicott, Bechdel, and Woolf in *Mothers: An Essay on Love and Cruelty*. Why, she asks, do we expect so much of mothers? Why do we expect them to carry our burdens? Why, she writes, 'do we expect mothers to subdue the very fears we ourselves have laid at their door?'

And I do want my mother to subdue my fears, not least this fear that in writing of her I am misrepresenting her, that however I honest I might attempt to be, I am forming a narrative based not on her life, but on mine. My mother left me gaps, and if I tell you about them, maybe it is simply a matter of filling them in. And yet, this ever-expanding constellation of texts seems like it must be true, it must tell me something about my mother, myself, my world.

I find the same sensation reading *The Secret Garden*. I remember my mother's excitement when she gave me the book, her hope that I would find myself in it, that I would see myself in Dickon, the young lad who talks to animals and knows how things grow. I had the same ruddy cheeks, certainly. But I did not see myself in Dickon, or in the sickly, spoiled child Colin, or in the angry, spoiled child Mary Lennox. When I read Frances Hodgson Burnett, I far preferred *The Little Princess*, because I wanted to be good, and kind, and orphaned, and saved. I wanted more than anything to be Sara Crewe, to find friends when I was friendless, to take pleasure in the company of rats and monkeys, to have, too, great misery and tales of woes. I wanted very much to go to a girls' boarding school. I wanted to be loveably sad, not irritatingly sad. *The Secret Garden* was too sentimental, and its miseries were not exciting enough.

I was wrong. The problem was that I, like my mother, was Mary. Mary Lennox is not a protagonist with whom the reader wishes to identify. She is, from the first sentence, 'the most disagreeable-looking child ever seen'. She is spoiled, she is snappish, she is alone. She is traumatised, in Winnicott's sense, where trauma is 'the breaking of the continuity of the line of the individual's existence'. The child whose home has failed to provide stability, Winnicott says, is often perceived to feel free, and yet this is not the case. He writes: 'Finding the framework of his life broken, he no longer feels free. He becomes anxious, and if he has hope he proceeds to look for a framework elsewhere than at home.'

When my mother's framework was broken, if it was ever whole, she sought other frameworks. Mary Lennox initially does not. There is a continuity, a loveless but stable home, that she simply attempts to transport to another country, another life, and it fails her entirely. It is not that her childhood in India is happy and the following years are unhappy, but that she, unlike the reader, does not understand that she never knew happiness at all, only the abuse of power. Mary, like my mother, grew up in a household without love, but she does not immediately understand why this is a problem. While it is certainly the case that many of the protagonists of the books I read are noted for their difference, for their sense of unbelonging, almost all of them quickly learn how to belong. Mary is the rare example of a heroine who makes a virtue of her nonbelonging, because it has never occurred to her that her life might be lived otherwise.

Perhaps it is unfair to compare my mother to Mary Lennox. In fact, given that my father is the one who grew up in India – if only for a few years – it seems particularly wrong to me. But Mary's loveless childhood and my mother's, however different their specifics, still seem similar. Both fight against the world because the world has already failed them.

The first chapters of *The Secret Garden* make sense to me only because I had already read *Jane Eyre*. If I couldn't warm to Mary, I could still sympathise with orphan girls being driven across the moors. There is no more romantic situation in my imagination, no setting in which I see myself more clearly. But the novel becomes stranger when we are finally introduced to Martha, the servant girl who is charged with looking after Mary, and Dickon's sister. For an American child in the late twentieth century, Martha's situation seems peculiar; she is quite content in servitude, her only pleasure one afternoon off a month when she returns home to cook and clean for her family instead of her employers. (Martha, certainly, has a good-enough mother.) And yet she is happy, happy enough that I retain a small juvenile crush on her to this day. But more than that, her speech is marked as different, both in sound and content. Her first lengthy quotation is in praise of the moors.

'I just love it. It's none bare. It's covered wi' growin' things as smells sweet. It's fair lovely in spring an' summer when th' gorse an' broom an' heather's in flower. It smells o' honey an' there's such a lot o' fresh air – an' th' sky looks so high an' th' bees an' skylarks makes such a nice noise hummin' an' singin'. Eh! I wouldn't live away from th' moor for anythin'.'

As a child I might not have known what gorse was, I might never have seen a skylark, and I'm sure I did not know why so many consonants appeared to have gotten lost along the way. But I could taste Martha's breathless excitement, those eight conjunctions carrying the reader along into a world that was not depicted, but imagined. The moor seems beautiful because Martha believes that it is. The entire framework for the rest of the novel is presented here, and the reader must succumb to it.

Mary takes a long time to succumb, and when she does, it is not because a human speaks to her, but a robin. Long before the idea of magic is introduced in the novel, the relations between humans and animals are already magical. It is a robin who shows Mary how to find the secret garden; the robin is the first person, or creature, to whom she shows affection. Dickon may tame foxes and crows, but even Mary finds companionship in nonhuman animals. Although Burnett does not anthropomorphise her animals to the same extent as Grahame, or even Adams, in their interactions with humans they are treated even more as equals. The animals are invested in the human world; they are agents of change, and are curious about affairs of the heart. Burnett balances a series of absent humans, including several dead mothers, against a menagerie of very present animals. Before the secret garden has even been entered, the world is already full and shared.

If in rereading many childhood books I have been surprised at just how many events are packed into the pages, returning to *The Secret Garden* makes me marvel at how much is deferred. Mary's discovery of the garden, her meeting Dickon, her eventual meeting of Colin, all take place later in the novel than the reader might expect. Instead, we spend a long time with Mary on her own, very gradually learning to love the world. The parallels between her life and the flowers in the garden, long hidden but able to thrive if given enough room to grow, are clear. But Burnett is also giving the reader a chance to learn to love Mary herself, to understand that even in this most disagreeable child there is a figure we can recognise. What happens 'under the dark earth', Burnett insists, is just as important as what happens above; what we see is only a small part of what surrounds us.

If Mary learns to love her bit of earth, it is just as important that she learns to incorporate her own experiences into her life; like the rabbits in *Watership Down*, she must learn how history and imagination combine to form a community. At the opening of the novel her memories of India are static, used only for comparison. She is not interested in books particularly; she is not allowed to use the library in England, and her only literary reference points are fairy tales, for which she has little time. When she meets Colin, however, she becomes a storyteller. He is like a rajah in India, she tells him, and Dickon is like a snake charmer. Her early childhood becomes a way of understanding the present, and of helping others to understand themselves. Rather than seeking a wholly new framework, she finds a way to extend one set of understanding into another. For the magic of Burnett's novel is not that Mary is transformed, but that she is transformed into someone she has always had the potential to be.

The final third of the novel might strike some readers as overly sentimental. Colin learns to walk, and to be a decent human being, and earns the love of his father. Mary also learns to be a decent human being, and earns the love of all around her. Dickon merely continues to be a sort of saint, at one point showing up with a lamb in his arms, a fox by his side, a crow on his shoulder, and a squirrel in his pocket. Allusions to magic appear more often; the garden is so transfigured that it seems 'as if Magicians were passing through it drawing loveliness out of the earth and the boughs with wands.' The children become, or feel, eternal.

And yet I cannot resist the magic Burnett describes. My mother's favourite film for all of my childhood was Franco Zeffirelli's *Brother Sun, Sister Moon*, a deeply romantic, counter-cultural story of St Francis of Assisi from 1972 and very much of its time, complete with Donovan soundtrack. When we finally bought a VCR it was one of the first films she sought out, and she made a sound-track of her own, positioning a microphone in front of the tele-vision and recording the entire thing, playing it on cassette over and over. I know every word of the film, every sound effect, every breath. At one point Francis has returned from the Crusades, and is ill. He hears a small bird, and walks along the peak of a roof to speak to it, crowds of passersby gathering below, afraid he will fall. To love animals, the film says, is a form of madness, and it is the only love that matters, because it allows the love of people as well. You begin your journey to health by loving just one bird. And while I do not know if Zeffirelli's film provided my mother with the understanding, the love, she needed, it did transform her in some way. And so too Burnett's novel, where the incorporation of every living thing into the text makes the world worthy of love.

Colin learns to observe the world around him.

If you watched long enough, he declared, you could see buds unsheathe themselves. Also you could make the acquaintance of strange, busy insect things running about on various unknown but evidently serious errands, sometimes carrying tiny scraps of straw or feather or food, or climbing blades of grass as if they were trees from whose tops one could look out to explore the country. A mole throwing up its mound at the end of its burrow and making its way out at last with the long-nailed paws, which looked so like elfish hands, had absorbed him one whole morning. Ants' ways, beetles' ways, frogs' ways, birds' ways, plants' ways, gave him a new world to explore, and, when Dickon revealed them all and added foxes' ways, otters' ways, ferrets' ways, squirrels' ways, and trouts' and water-rats' and badgers' ways, there was no end to the things to talk about and think over.

This is too much of a peaceable kingdom, not least when the children band together and sing the doxology – Praise God from whom all blessings flow – a song I sang at least weekly as a child. It is too much, the world is too rich, we are too broken to accept it. And yet, for a moment, I do. If *Charlotte's Web* is the story of how one can make a good life in the face of one's own mortality, *The Secret Garden* is the story of what one does when 'one is quite sure one is going to live for ever and ever and ever'. To be part of everything, to attend to the world as it is and as it is inhabited, is a way of extending the self beyond the confines of an individual life.

Some years after Burnett's novel an Estonian environmental scientist named Jakob von Uexküll would develop a view of the world not dissimilar to Colin's. It is a mistake, he says, to say there is one world and that we see it correctly. It is a mistake to say that there is a universal sense of space and of time, a right way of relating to the world. We each relate to the world differently. In a 1940 text translated as *A Theory of Meaning* he gives the example of a blooming meadow flower, and asks the reader to imagine it from the perspective of a girl picking the flower for a bouquet, an ant walking across the stem, a spittle-bug larva that lives within the stem, and a cow who eats the flower. The same flower, he says, is decorative, functional, home, and food. There is no objective, single world out there; the world is as we perceive it, as we experience it, and that this experience is partial is no detriment to our understanding.

This is the same world that Colin sees. The busy insects, the mole, and the child occupy the same world, but no one perspective on it is truer than the others, no one person, or species, has control over the narrative. This is the same world of multiple sensory experiences we find in White's farm, the same flexible environment we find on Grahame's river bank, the same exploration we find in Adams's rabbits. This is why animal stories matter: they tell us that the world is not for us alone, that it is only when we begin to imagine the world from another perspective that we can find who we are, in ourselves and in community. Animal stories matter because they show us that we are enmeshed in a living, vibrant world, and that our ideas of hierarchy, of rules, of differentiation are mistaken. They teach us how to be with others.

And so the novel's happy, sentimental end does not trouble me. It is too easy to read the story as simply a tale of how broken people can heal themselves if they spend enough time in a garden, although that does not stop me from longing for a garden even now. It is, instead, a tale of how being broken does not define you, does not remove you from the world. It is a story of how we are all broken, and this can be a point of connection.

My mother was broken. She was, I believe, broken in more ways than I will ever know. And yet she kept insisting she could find a way to see the world anew, from a different perspective.

My mother loved *The Secret Garden*. As much as our move to Vermont was based on the search for human community, I believe it was just as much based on her desire to have a bit of earth of her own, to make something grow, to live in, or to invent, her own peaceable kingdom.

My mother was just as moved by Annie Dillard's observations of the natural world, the need to look closely, and in that looking, to see things as they are, and as they transcend our own partial view. Her copy of Dillard's short text *Holy the Firm* was a Christmas present from my uncle in 1977. It is the book in which I keep the prayer cards that were handed out at her funeral; it is the first thing I would save in a fire; I have kept it next to my bed for twenty years.

There are two fires in Dillard's book. The first is that of a moth, who burns, horrifically, in a candle, and whose body then becomes a wick. The fire is first threat, and real death, and then a form of continuance, and even beauty. The second fire is a burned child, a neighbour named Julie Norwich – and Dillard, even if drawing on her own life, could not have been unaware of the closeness to Julian of Norwich. Julie Norwich has been burned in an accident; she is scarred. Dillard searches for meaning in this suffering; she wants to find something transfiguring, something meaningful, some sense of persistent beauty. And Dillard speaks to Julie Norwich, at the book's end, in epiphanic terms, telling her that she is 'held fast by the love in the world like the moth in wax, your life a wick, your head on fire with prayer.' 'So live,' she writes. 'I'll be the nun for you. I am now.'

We burn. We are alone. We are transfigured.

There are no solutions in Dillard's essay. There is no moment when the universe coheres as it does in Burnett's novel, there is no happy ending, no comforting moral. The child's pain cannot be assuaged by beautiful sentences. But Dillard posits watching as important as living, prayer as important as action, the human as important as the animal, death as important as life.

The world is so splendid that perhaps we can learn to love it best when we are broken. And this does not mean we must romanticise our brokenness, but rather it means we must accept that it is our foundation. Our broken bodies, our broken frameworks for living, are what bring us into a love of the world.

Woolf makes the same point, or a similar one, in 'The Death of a Moth', where she describes a single, dying moth, hurling himself against a window, as 'little or nothing but life', part of the 'same energy which inspired the rooks, the ploughmen, the horses, and even, it seemed, the lean bare-backed downs' outside. The moth is full of life, and then is dead; it is not an allegory, but simply the nature of experience. And yet to witness this moth is meaningful. To see the world, to see the stake each creature has in it, is to understand our own place in it, and our own failings. The death of this one moth is all deaths, but its life is all life.

My mother was abused. But this did not define her. She was unloved, and yet she loved, and became loved. She was alone, and she was enmeshed in an endlessly rich world. She was lonely. She lived.

The Book of the Dun Cow

On 10 December 1978, less than three weeks before I was born, *The New York Times* ran a lengthy review by Robert Kiely of a first novel by an American minister, Walter Wangerin, Jr., under the heading 'A Fable for Our Time'. The reviewer insists that Wangerin's novel, *The Book of the Dun Cow*, must appear, in its focus on farm-yard animals, 'as bizarre as any intergalactic melodrama'. What could children who have never seen a pig or a rabbit make of a story in which all the characters are animals, Kiely wonders. This is not like *Winnie-the-Pooh* or *Charlotte's Web*, the critic says, since the first is really only the story of a toy, and the latter is no more than a digested version of *The Power of Positive Thinking*. (A large advert for White's novel placed opposite Kiely's review indicates a sub-editor with a sense of humour, at least.) This is, instead, a 'painfully violent and bleak book' that carries echoes of Auschwitz, Hiroshima, and Vietnam.

The Book of the Dun Cow was heralded at the time. It was recognised as 'A Best Children's Book of the Year' by *The New York Times* and 'A Best Book for Children' by the *School Library Journal*. In 1980, when the National Book Awards briefly rebranded and added a number of new categories, it won the award for 'Best Science Fiction Paperback', an award never given before or again. Contemporary reviews compare it favourably to J. R. R. Tolkien, to George Orwell, to Richard Adams. And it has all but vanished since; I have not met anyone, even of my generation, even of those who shopped in Christian bookstores in the 1980s, who has read it. But it, and its strange sequel *The Book of Sorrows* – a book so relent-lessly grim that the version currently in print has been expurgated by Wangerin himself and published under a new title – provided a common language for my family. The cry of the self-hating outcast dog Mundo Cani, 'Marooooooooooned', was echoed weekly.

These books do not have remotely happy endings. They are phenomenally violent. They have much to say about the nature of guilt. It is painful to return to them.

The Book of the Dun Cow is about a rooster, Chauntecleer – misspelled on the cover of my British edition from 1990 – and his wife Pertelote, names taken from Chaucer's 'The Nun's Priest's Tale', as are several of the incidents of the story. They live in a farmyard with many other animals, familiar from many children's stories, although human characters are completely absent. They have been charged to protect the earth from a great Wyrm who lives beneath the ground, large enough to circle the globe. They are not successful. Although the farm setting, and the species of all of the animals described, are familiar from other children's books, there is no sense of an outside world in which the reader could place themselves; there is only cosmic struggle.

At the start of the novel Wyrm is angry, in his earthly prison, and visits an old rooster on another farm, Senex, who then lays an egg, which hatches to reveal a half-chicken, half-snake creature called Cockatrice. Cockatrice and a Toad then rape the other hens – this is a very curious and disturbing children's book, I cannot lie – and give birth to a host of basilisks, who eventually attack the farm of good animals, beginning a war that occupies the majority of the novel. This is not, Wangerin cautions, an allegory; it is fundamentally a tale of good and evil, and the evil in the novel is grotesque. The good, however, is not so appealing either. Chauntecleer is vain and preening, and he is unable to win against the forces of evil. Wangerin delights in his description of the 'wasted land, the shattered society, the bodies dead and festering'; the deaths of the various animals are detailed and gruesome. At last Chauntecleer fights and defeats Cockatrice, and yet the war is not over, and this is where the novel becomes interesting.

Mundo Cani, the dog, the dog of the world, has been an irritation to Chauntecleer throughout the novel. He speaks endlessly of his ugliness, his misery; he arrives at the farm at the novel's opening, and while each of the animals is moved to pity as he howls his loneliness and grief, they also long for his silence and departure. He is a comic foil, a sort of Uriah Heep without the intelligence or cunning. And he saves the world. When Chauntecleer is too wounded to fight on, Mundo Cani challenges Wyrm himself, precisely because of his insignificance: ' "Wyrm, look at me! Wyrm, see me! A Dog! A Dog! A nothing to look upon!" ' He stabs Wyrm in the eye with the horn of the Dun Cow, a figure of peace, and descends into the pit, like Prometheus, like Christ, and yet without the nobility of either. And Chauntecleer is inconsolable; the war which was his to win has been won, or temporarily ended, by a strange, unlovable dog. The moral of the story might be, as the *New York Times* critic states, that one does not need to be Christ-like to perform a Christian act, but this is not sufficient as a reading, for the reader does not understand, or sympathise, with Mundo Cani, but rather with the suffering, ineffectual Chauntecleer. His wife speaks to him of sacrifice, of penance, and yet he is not restored; he cannot understand how a battle between good and evil can be ended by a figure who speaks only of loss. And there the novel ends.

Wangerin picks up the tale seven years later in *The Book of Sorrows*. While the first book was often read aloud in my childhood, this one was read only once for, as my parents commented, it is a book that deserves its title. It is not a good novel, if such categorisations are important; there are too many characters, often indistinguishable, and the entire arc of the story is Chauntecleer's guilt and self-hatred. It is as unpleasant a novel as I have ever encountered. Of course I read it to myself many times.

Melanie Klein, the psychoanalyst from whom Winnicott learned much, and from whom he sought to distance himself, places aggression at the heart of the child–parent relationship. Her work is rooted in case histories and, as when I read Freud, I am suspicious when I read it. There is too much anality, too many genitalia, and I refuse to see myself in it. Her essay 'Love, Guilt and Reparation', from 1937, is different. The sources are often literary, odd insertions of Romantic poetry. And what she says seems to me extraordinarily true. Infancy, she says, is a struggle between love and hate, and when we hate those who love us, we feel guilty. When we make sacrifices for the person we love, when we identify with them, we play the part of a good parent. If we are not able to do so, we turn away.

Klein is more hopeful here than in other essays, and argues that the desire to rediscover our mother, to forgive and to sacrifice, to make peace, is central to creative art, and that it can liberate us. 'If we have become able, deep in our unconscious minds, to clear our feelings to some extent towards our parents of grievances, and have forgiven them for the frustrations we had to bear, then we can be at peace with ourselves and are able to love others in the true sense of the word', she writes.

Have I forgiven my mother? Did she forgive her parents? Can Chauntecleer forgive Mundo Cani, forgive himself?

I was a difficult teenager. At some point, for years, I became obsessed with my own guilt. I would leap up from the dinner table and bang my head against the wall, shouting 'I'm sorry! I'm sorry!' For years my parents tried to get me to stop using 'sorry' as a linguistic filler, in place of 'um' or 'ah'. I was so sorry, all the time. And I couldn't stop. I couldn't not be sorry. I would pace back and forth in the kitchen, the living room, caught in an unending loop of self-hatred and self-pity.

I didn't know, most of the time, what I was sorry for. Sorry for being in the world, sorry for taking up space, sorry for not loving enough.

And sometimes I had real reasons to be sorry. In the early winter of 1994, probably February, I cut off my mother's finger. When I tell this story now I try to make it a joke. I rarely succeed. I was on my way to a musical audition, since the classical guitar was central to my life at the time. And for some reason I needed to stop in, on the way, to the bookstore I worked at; I'd forgotten something, left something behind, something was urgent, something was needed. And we parked the car behind the bookstore, in the icy Harmony Lot, and I ran off, shutting the rear passenger door hard behind me. My mother, of course, hated ice, felt unsteady, and her hand was on the bar between the rear and front passenger seats.

I had, a week or two before, seen Jane Campion's film *The Piano*. And as I knelt on the pavement, looking for the part of my mother's finger I had severed, I could think of nothing else. I did not find it. And I did not do well on that audition.

My mother had played the guitar too, folk rather than classical, playing and singing in a string of folk groups at church services. She was not an accomplished guitarist, but she enjoyed it, and she enjoyed that, although we played different styles, we shared this. And, no longer possessing all of her fingers, she could not continue.

She was surprisingly resilient. Within a few months she had decided to play the fiddle instead, since the shortened finger was on what became her bowing hand. And for the rest of her life, her fiddle was her greatest solace, her greatest entertainment. She played Scottish folk and Appalachian, learning from scratch. She spent so much time in violin stores that my father, when he retired from stone and brick masonry, went into violin repair, simply because while waiting for her he had begun to wonder how the instruments worked.

The last time I saw my mother, she sold her violin, exchanging it for a guitar I loved. We bought the guitar on a Thursday, and shipped it to Scotland. I arrived back in my student flat there on the Monday, the guitar on the Tuesday, and I called her to thank her. I do not remember ending our conversation by saying 'I love you', and yet I must have done, for I had said goodbye like that every day for years, knowing that one of our conversations would be the last. She was dead twenty-four hours later. We buried her ashes in her violin case.

And I am sorry.

But I was sorry, too, for so many other things. I was sorry for surviving, when I knew she wouldn't. I was sorry that I could not save her. And I still am. I was sorry that I wasn't enough, and more than that, sorry that I could not be as happy as she wanted me to be.

Chauntecleer is sorry too, in *The Book of Sorrows*. For much of the novel he reflects on the problem of evil, he considers his own failings, he wonders about the utility of the rituals that he is charged with maintaining. He searches for forgiveness, which he believes he can only find in sacrifice. And so he decides to find out what happened to Wyrm and Mundo Cani, to avenge the latter and kill the former. He will be glorious in battle, and good will finally triumph over evil. And, quite late in the novel, he too descends into the depths, and he is horrified by what he finds. For Wyrm is dead, and has been all along. All that is left is 'a marsh of rot', 'an oily, putrefying meat'. He cannot be vindicated, he cannot sacrifice himself. And Mundo Cani, too, is dead.

Here the novel becomes even more curious, and more distressing. Chauntecleer is infected with little worms that have been living on, or hatched from, Wyrm's corpse. And they turn his mind. He drags the skull of the dog back to the farmyard, but he has become cruel and selfish; he brings, inadvertently, evil back into the world, simply because he believes it has never left. And he realises what his final act must be, which is to slit his own stomach open, releasing the parasitical worms. He does so. He dies. The end.

The moral of the story, such as it is, is not simply that there is no final triumph of good over evil. Chauntecleer is not Aslan, victorious in death, nor is he Charlotte, willingly giving her life. He is a small, petty man – or rooster – who cannot be the person he wishes, and who cannot accept that great good may be done by those of whom it is least expected.

I hate reading this novel, but I empathise. Because after the period in which I was sorry, I ran, as Klein would predict.

I left home at sixteen, to college in New York, a move that my mother would later say saved our relationship. I moved to Scotland, to Boston, and back to Scotland again. I tried to be a scientist, a bookseller, a filmmaker, and became an academic in the end. There were years I moved flat every month, and years

I stagnated, living in places I was unhappy because I could not conceive of change.

I fell in love, and was loved in return. I was a terrible boyfriend. Several times I came out of the closet, looked around, and went back in, like some sort of sexual identity groundhog. I cared about my career; I read thousands of books, some of them about animals. I sold books and I taught books and I made books my entire life. I continued to play the guitar for a time, and then gave it up. I was happy and unhappy, like anybody else; my life was no better or worse than I made it. I made good choices and bad choices and most of all I failed to choose. But every moment of it was running.

And my mother did not run, in the nine final years of her life, when I was away. I spoke to her every day, and yet it is hard to know exactly what her life entailed. Her health diminished. Her mobility decreased, she developed astounding headaches, she had fewer and fewer friends. She played music, and developed a lasting love of the Catholic church, and was invested in a community wholly, permanently, for one of the first times in her life. And yet I do not know, somehow, what she was thinking all those years, whether or not she was happy. I have long passed the age my mother was when I left home, and I should be able to see her now more clearly, and I cannot. At her funeral people spoke of how funny she was, how smart, how idiosyncratic, and they said that they wished they had seen her more recently, that they'd kept in touch.

The week I left for college my mother took apart my childhood bedroom, as I would not need it any more. She painted it and replaced the bed, removed all the detritus of my high-school years. But she and my father also began to make a new room, a special room, at the end of the house, in what had always been a derelict space. It is a simple room, with exposed beams and yellow walls, a beautiful fireplace in the corner, a cupboard my mother painted with images from Tolkien. It is, precisely, the room you see on the packaging for Celestial Seasonings Sleepytime Tea, with its bears in their pyjamas.

The current design for the tea shows a father bear, presumably, in front of the fireplace, a radio by his side, a cat at his feet. The version from the 1980s, which we had as part of a set of placemats, is larger. There is the father, the cat, the radio, and a large clock. A bird sits over the fireplace, and there is a pot of tea at the father's side. But there is a whole world to the left of the image as well. A toy bear, on wheels, a painting of a polar bear on the wall. There is a mother bear, too, her face turned towards the open door to the next room. In her left arm she carries the littlest bear, already asleep, while a slightly older cub, in a pink dress, looks back at her snoozing father, wanting just another moment with him.

In our identical room, my mother was in the father's place. It was, at last, a room of her own. It was a room in which she played the violin, in which she read, in which she watched her small collection of films. It was the room in which she died. The first thing my father did that night was to stop the clock, there in its ordained place, and it was not wound again for years. It is the room in which I sleep when I visit my father now, on the sofa, to be close to the fire. But I am fascinated, looking at this advertising image now, by the departing family, because I am, if anyone, the girl cub, looking back to the warmth, to the light, and being taken away.

I am so happy my mother had a room of her own, even if it was not one in which she was ever able to write. I am happy she had a place to find solace.

Because the thing is, I lied, right at the start of this story. I told you funerals were easy. But no, they are always hard. The service went smoothly. A local fiddler played a version of 'Ashokan Farewell', one of my mother's favourite songs – you'll remember it from the soundtrack of the Ken Burns documentary on the American Civil War – far better than my mother ever could. And then the eulogy began. And the priest recounted my mother's final words, the only time I have ever heard them: 'What do people who feel this bad do?'

'What do people who feel this bad do?'

Because I now know not only that my mother died in pain, but that she lacked words for that pain. That she ended her life with a question she could not answer. And since that day there is scarcely a moment when those words do not still ring in my ears, where I do not want to find an answer, when I do not want, somehow, to make everything better, to be the hero in the story, to save her from all hardship and pain.

My father decided that my mother did not need an autopsy. Had she had a stroke or died of kidney failure? Had it been the cervical cancer, the diabetes, the high blood pressure? We did not need to know, in the end. She died of too much pain, of having lived too long already. No doctor could give us an answer to the questions that remained, no diagnosis would suffice.

The essay that immediately follows 'Love, Guilt and Reparation' in the volume of Klein's by my side is titled 'Mourning and its Relation to Manic-Depressive States', and it is a retort to, or a development of, Freud's work on 'Mourning and Melancholia'. The infant, Klein states, incorporates their parents within their body; the parents become internal or inner objects, part of the child's unconscious fantasies. And the terrible thing about mourning, Klein argues, is not simply that you have lost the external object, the loved person who lived and moved and had their being in the world, but that you lose your internal 'good' object as well. Recovery, for Klein, is learning to reinstate these good objects, and depression arises when you cannot. This, for Klein, is the true work of mourning. It is not a novel act that arises only when it is needed. It is a repetition of what we did as infants. She says that for the one who has lost what they loved, the work of mourning is a matter of 'recovering what he had already attained in childhood'.

This is why I have to go back to the books I read in childhood, in the order that I read them. It is only in this reading and rereading that I can begin the work of recovery, work I have deferred for almost fifteen years. It is only because these books had explanatory power then that they have explanatory power now.

This is a standard argument for those who study children's literature. Valerie Krips argues in *The Presence of the Past* that we 'are never free of our past', but we are 'fully capable of reimaging it and renarrativizing it; thus, when we come across a book we loved as a child, we meet it from a long perspective, with the accretions of time and socialization upon us'. Margaret Mackey makes a not dissimilar argument in *One Child Reading* that we 'do not learn to read in the abstract', but 'in grounded, individual, and local times and spaces'. That is, we read in particulars, not universals, and we return to our reading with a whole new set of particular experiences. Our past is known in repetition and return; it is known in its specifics, in its specific moments and rooms and the books we held in them. And we can incorporate those experiences, we can find our way back.

But we do more than that. The books we love are external objects and internal ones as well. We love and hate them, and we incorporate them into ourselves. And if we reread as an act of mourning, we must learn to reinstate these stories as internal objects. We need to reacquire them, to recreate them. To rediscover what we have lost, we must rediscover what we have loved.

My mother always saw herself in books, sometimes in the most literal fashion. In the kitchen there was a shelf of reference books, mostly cookbooks, some field guides, and above all *The Merck Manual*, a great tome of symptoms and diagnoses for every conceivable ailment. Every malady, hers and mine, was referred to the manual. As a child I was sure that this was simply the behaviour of a hypochondriac, but I see now that it was a form of control, of integration, a way of looking for an explanatory narrative. Opening the *Merck* was a way of going to an already-known text and finding something new in it, something pertinent, something true. It was a way for my mother to take control of her life, to be an authority on her own existence, rather than an object for medical study. The ability to diagnose was the ability to tell a story about yourself, one that mattered.

But it was not just the *Merck*. It was true of every cookbook, every volume of poetry, every theological tract: somewhere on the page was a solution. There was a story that could explain everything, if only you kept reading.

Winnicott writes about this, too, in an extraordinary essay from 1948, 'Reparation in Respect of Mother's Organized Defence against Depression.' He writes about mothers who seem too aware of medical symptoms, who bring their children to the doctor because they themselves may be depressed. And then he reverses it – for the appeal of Winnicott is that he is not a misogynist – and states, curiously, that 'The child uses the mother's depression as an escape from his or her own.' It is not that the parent dominates the child, he asserts, but that the child lives within the circle of their parents' personality. Dealing with their mother's moods, he says, is the only way of 'creating an atmosphere in which they can *start on their own lives*', but within that, he writes, there can be a simultaneous 'flight from that acceptance of personal responsibility which is an essential part of individual development'.

A person's guilt, their need for reparation, he concludes, may not be their own, but might be instead their response to the depression of their parents. But the story they tell of their parents' depression may be a way of not looking at their own.

I know that my mother was depressed, in my childhood, in the years after. Some nights, when I was pretending to be asleep, I heard her tell my father how much she wanted to die. I know that she felt an enormous sense of guilt at times, although I do not know the cause. I know that her parents' depressions affected her enormously. I dealt with her moods as well, as poorly, as any child might; I consoled when I could, I was callous when I couldn't. I made an attempt to start on my own life, and I fled responsibility.

And this is the appeal of Wangerin's text for me. It does not explain my mother, but it explains some of my own life, my own need to pay reparation, my own guilt. And if Wangerin cannot provide a happy ending, perhaps I can do better. Because I need to tell you that my mother was depressed, yes, but that she was dedicated to teaching herself what she needed to know to save her life. She made herself an authority because she had to. She was lonely, yes, and she was angry, and she fought, every day, for herself, for me, for my father. She was funny. She was in love. She was terrified. She could not bear the world she was presented, and so she kept trying to make a new one. She made, as Simone de Beauvoir says of her own mother, a world 'whose whole existence was caused by her being there'. And her life was miraculous.

In the immediate aftermath of her death, my father referred to my mother as a saint. I recoiled: she was too much part of the world, of my world, to hold at such a remove. But where my father was right, I think, is in evoking that now old-fashioned, religiously tinted notion of grace. My mother lived by grace. She lived by love. She knew her own part of the world.

The Man Who Was Magic

It's another year in my childhood; I'm maybe eight or nine, and again I'm sick. And my mother brings me a book she loved as a child, because she believes I will see myself in it. The book is called *The Abandoned*. It is a story about cats.

The book is better known in Britain by the title *Jennie*, and remains moderately well known, in part because of the success of its author Paul Gallico's earlier fable of the Second World War, *The Snow Goose*. Gallico was an American who lived for parts of his life in Britain, and was enormously popular, and enormously prolific, although he has since fallen out of fashion. And yet his work appears in the oddest places. 'Farida's Eyes', by the Sudanese/ Scottish writer Leila Aboulela tells the story of a young child whose education is hampered because her father believes glasses will make her ugly. The book she is unable to read at school, in an unspecified location that is likely Khartoum, is Gallico's novel *Flowers for Mrs Harris*; the children find the idea of any similarity between the Parisian setting of that text and their own lives hilarious. Besides *The Snow Goose* Gallico is perhaps most famous as the author of *The Poseidon Adventure*, a novel about a horrible accident on a cruise ship that became one of the first star-studded disaster films of the 1970s, and which gave me as many childhood nightmares as *The Story of Babar*. *Jennie* is less sentimental than *The Snow Goose*, and less camp than *The Poseidon Adventure*, but it still makes me cry.

At the start of the novel Peter, a boy about my own age at the time, has an accident when he goes to pet a kitten in the street; he awakes to find himself apparently unharmed, but gradually realises that he has taken on the form of a cat, despite retaining the consciousness and memories of his life as a boy. Thrown into the street, he has to learn how to navigate his new body, and is helped by a tabby he meets named Jennie Baldrin. Jennie is teacher, mother, and lover all at once. She washes Peter, teaches him how to eat mice and fight rats, and how to behave in ways that are appropriately feline. What makes the novel unusual among literary transformation stories is that neither human nor feline behaviours are privileged; both worlds are constructed around a series of rules, some practical, some more arbitrary, that have to be learned. There is little sense that either species is superior, or more rooted in place, or more observant; rather, cats and humans are shown to have similar challenges, but different solutions. If children's books are always, to some extent, a matter of socialisation, of teaching the reader how to be in the world, Gallico indicates the way every society has its own particular customs.

Jennie and Peter are both abandoned; Peter's greatest fear is that he will never again find his human mother, while Jennie has been removed from her original Scottish home and has had to live on the streets of London. Their adventures range from finding a temporary home in a theatrical scenery warehouse to a sea voyage to Glasgow; they meet kind and cruel cats and humans alike. Perhaps the saddest story, though, is that of Mr Grims, an old man who lives by himself on the docks. Grims has 'the mildest blue eyes that Peter had ever seen, eyes that had in them a look of great kindliness and at the same time sadness'. Grims shares what little he has with the cats, but Jennie is suspicious, believing that Grims is only kind to the two cats because he wants something from them, and the cats flee. After their Glasgow expedition, however, Jennie relents, accepting that Grims could provide them with a good home, and Peter is delighted. When they return they find Grims asleep, with 'an extraordinary sweetness about the mouth' and a 'gentle manner in which the closed eyelids lay over the eyes that Peter knew contained so much kindliness'. For Grims is not asleep, but dead, himself abandoned and alone.

The story is ultimately about the ways that empathy crosses species boundaries. Jennie loves Peter, Peter loves Jennie, and Grims loves them both. None of these loves relies on complete understanding; each individual's experience is unique, and however many stories they share, no one party wholly understands the other. And yet the emotions they all feel are real. The way a cat loves is not so different, in the end, from the way a human loves, and the purpose of the novel is to teach the reader that these loves are real, that they matter. Work in philosophy and science has similarly begun to recognise, in recent years, the importance, the reality, of animal emotions. Carl Safina, for instance, argues that 'deciding that other animals can't have any emotions that humans feel is a cheap way to get a monopoly on all the world's feelings and motivations. People who've systematically watched or known animals realize the absurdity of this.' To restrict our understanding of emotion to a particular form of language use, or a particular set of behaviours, seems foolish at best.

And, of course, we know this. We know from the animals around us that they have profound emotions. No one, perhaps, felt my mother's death more deeply than our dog, Pippin, who waited for her every day for the rest of his life. We know that animals suffer, that they mourn, that they love. And yet we do not have the language for this. We begin with the idea that human emotions and ways of understanding the world are in some sense right, and we test animals to see if they understand things the same way we do. We begin with the idea that the human understanding of the world is objectively correct, and position our own responses as both knowable and proper. As Vinciane Despret says in *What Would Animals Say If We Asked the Right Questions?*, in a discussion of chimpanzee mourning, the only way through is to 'put our own concepts to the test'. We have to begin to understand the world from the premise that our own ways of thinking and feeling are not preordained, that they are not whole. We have to accept that other forms of life, other ways of perceiving, have as much validity as our own, as much as we are still confined by human ways of understanding. Who else, asks Jenny Diski, 'can define suffering but humans? It's our word.' It is hard to imagine a way of understanding animals except through a human prism.

And this is the beauty of Gallico's book. He does not begin from the presumption that the human way of knowing is the right one. And of course it's all a construct, it is all a tale told by a human, and yet it brings the reader into an understanding of love, of empathy, and of suffering. Gallico does not worry, overtly, about the dangers of anthropocentrism, or the tricks that language plays. He asserts, instead, that all creaturely life is made of this relation between love and suffering. Our lives, all of our lives, human and animal alike, are formed in relation to others, and in our own abandonment.

It would be trite to say that the reason we read children's books is to know why it is that we suffer, and yet what unites these books from my childhood is their profound sense of loneliness, at times, and from this loneliness the discovery that even the abandoned can enter into a community. I like to think this is why my mother gave me Gallico's book to read. She saw in me someone who was lonely, and perhaps she remembered her own loneliness, and she saw that reading the story of those who were also lonely could be a way out.

The Scottish novelist A. L. Kennedy talks about how we write out of love. 'We all meet our ends', she says, 'happily or sadly and sooner or later, but in this way of helping each other, in this manifestation of joy and hope and kindness, we also have a kind of immortality. And we need never be alone.' Writing, even reading, is how we find our way out of loneliness. It is how we make our own absence, our own loss, present and material.

My mother gave me books because they would help me. I read them now as a way of trying to reach into the past, and help her. And maybe we are still alone, and yet we partake in this larger community. We are there on the Glasgow docks and in the London streets, we are there as cats and people, we are there loving and fearing the world together. And we are there not just in one book, but all of them. We are on the river bank and in the jungle, on farms and in towns. We are rabbits and squirrels, pigs and chickens. We are more than human, more than ourselves, and so we know, for a moment, who we are.

As a child I thought *Jennie*'s ending was cheating. Peter is separated from Jennie, and falls in love, disastrously, and has a fight with another cat, and almost dies. And he wakes up as a human, and Jennie is gone; he hears what he believes is her voice, and it becomes the voice of his mother. He is human again. And nothing has distressed me more, as a reader, than the realisation that the entirety of a narrative may have been no more than a dream. It was what I always disliked about the Alice books, what still frustrates me about John Masefield's *The Box of Delights*, why all the fancy of the film version of *The Wizard of Oz* seemed pointless. The bond between Peter and Jennie is ruptured, and this seemed cruel to me; the reader is thrust back into the human world, as if to say this was the world that always mattered.

But I think I was wrong. For if Jennie disappears, the world Peter inhabited is still there. He is given a kitten and thrusts her away, for only Jennie can satiate his emotional needs. And the kitten, rejected, cries out.

He understood and he knew – oh, not what she was actually saying, for with his return to being a boy all knowledge of the language of cats had been wiped from his memory as thought it had never existed. But he recognised the wistful melody of the plaintive little mew, the cry of the waif, the stray, the unloved, and the homeless that he had come to know so well. It was the forlorn and lonely heart begging to be taken to his own, there to be warmed and cherished.

In it, he felt was contained all of the misery, hurt, and longing he seemed to have known for so long, and, for a moment, harsh, vivid memories of things that had happened to him and places where he had been during his illness came back for the last time.

Maybe this strikes you as too sentimental. But for myself, I do not know what literature is for if it is not to connect us to the voices of the lost, of the lonely, of those who fear and mourn.

Life, reading, is what teaches us that our own losses can be shared. And it teaches us that there is no final loss: there will always be new departures, there will always be new forms of suffering, and we must cling to what we have, because it is only in doing so that we can retrieve our own past. I still miss Jennie, at the end of the novel, but I understand what Gallico means, because what he describes here is, curiously, the same process Klein describes. Attending to the kitten is what allows Peter to reinstate Jennie as the internal loved object. 'The cry of the waif', Gallico writes, 'had made it possible just once more for him to peer through the closing door into that other world he had left for ever'. And while he loses Jennie, and loses her entire world – for every loss of a loved one is the loss of an entire world – he is able to internalise that love, that loss, and so to turn his love outward again.

I do not know if this is the lesson my mother intended for me, or if she intended a lesson at all. But it is, perhaps, the lesson I need now. If I do not have my mother's stories, I still have the stories she loved, and I can know her through them.

For years after my mother's death I repeated to myself a simple mantra, over and over: 'You will lose everything you love'. It became a comfort to know that loss was inevitable, rather than accidental; it became a way of feeling that I was prepared.

It took me years to realise that there was a second half to the equation: 'but you may find it again'.

The Gallico book my mother truly loved, and that I have also loved, past all reason, was published slightly later, in 1966, and is called *The Man Who Was Magic*. Its subtitle, 'A Fable of Innocence', might already make readers wary, and in America it was never reprinted. I have bought many copies over the years; the one I hold on to may or may not have been my mother's as a child, but is distinguished by my own illustrated cover, which my mother has laminated, depicting the novel's finale. It is not a very good illustration, and it is very dear to me; the book sits next to Dillard's on my bedside table.

Because you do not know the story – unless we dated, in which case I probably gave you a copy – let me tell you.

There is a town called Mageia, known for its magicians. Every magician in the world is based there, and it is the home of all the tricks of the trade. And one day a man, named simply Adam, appears, asking to audition for the magicians' guild. He is dressed simply, accompanied by his dog Mopsy, and carrying a simple staff. He has come from Glimour, beyond the Mountains of Straen, a journey which no one has undertaken before, and which no one believes possible. And he can do magic. Not tricks, not sleight-of-hand, not illusion, but magic.

Told he must acquire an assistant, he happens upon an eleven-and-a-half-year old girl, Jane, the exact age of my mother when the book was published. Jane is the daughter of the Great Robert, mayor of the city and chief magician. She is lonely. She has been, to some extent, abused. And Adam begins to show her, and all the town, his magic. His first trick is to unscramble an egg, and the other magicians, unable to see how he has done it, are suspicious and astonished. He helps a hapless magician known as Ninian the Nonpareil, who is both grateful and angry. For no one can understand how magic is possible, and if magic is possible, it will destroy the careers of every one of the stage magicians who live in the town.

A plot is hatched to kill Adam, by the rather appropriately named Malvolio. Almost all the town magicians conspire, even the hapless Ninian, for they know that not just their livelihoods but their very identities are at stake. And in his final performance, Adam remakes the world. He and Jane appear on a bare stage, Mopsy having been imprisoned. He places his clothes upon a rack, and appears unadorned. The stage is silent. And Adam makes a motion, a small motion. And out of his tailcoat comes a dove, and then another, and another, and the theatre is full of birds, 'tits and goldfinches, robins, larks, chaffinches, canaries, flycatchers, bullfinches, budgereegahs, greenfinches, honeysuckers, warblers, hummingbirds, chiffchaffs, bulbuls, small thrushes, cardinals, orioles and buntings'. The room is alive with colour, with sound.

And then butterflies. More butterflies than anyone has ever seen, so many that Adam and Jane become invisible. The world is full of colour and beauty.

It is this image that I chose for the cover of the book.

And then he gives the people what they want. Money of every currency and denomination falls from the roof. There is a stampede, there is injury, there is wealth. And Adam vanishes.

This is almost the entire novel. A stranger appears. He makes the world beautiful. He leaves. This is the story of everyone we have loved. This is Woolf's mother, this is mine. Ninian, at the novel's end, leaves the town behind, hoping to follow Adam, to make his amends, to pay his reparation. In this sense, Gallico is telling a story much like Wangerin's, the story of surprising beauty and sacrifice, and the guilt of those left behind.

But it is not the same story at all. For within the novel there are miracles. First, there is Mopsy, the talking dog. The reader is presented with long conversations between Adam and Mopsy, and so we know, or we presume we know, that Mopsy can speak. Yet no one else can hear the dog's voice, no one else has access to his thoughts. Mopsy is a secret that Adam and the reader share, because storytelling is, of course, just another form of magic. And yet Jane, although she cannot hear Mopsy's voice, loves him anyway, and he loves her. And he tells Adam, he tells the reader, of his love, and she does not know this as well as we do, and yet she must live with the presumption of that love.

And Adam also gives Jane her own form of magic. And it is a form we know well, if we have read White, if we have read Burnett.

Midway through the novel Jane and Adam go on a picnic, to a farm just outside the city gates. They are accompanied by Ninian, who is attempting to learn the secrets of Adam's magic, and spied on by Jane's brother, whom Adam dispenses with a cloud of hornets and wasps. The farm itself is a pastoral idyll, completely familiar from so many stories we read in youth.

There were horses poking their heads from several of the stalls in the stables below; sheep in a pasture with their fluffy, wobbly legged, young lambs stumbling about; cows in a green field on the opposite hillside and a flourishing kitchen garden. At one end of the farmyard was a pigsty with a number of pigs rolling happily in the mud, or scratching themselves against the sharp corners of the boards. At the other was a pond fed by the brook that came out of the woods not far from the hill. Ducks and ducklings, geese and goslings sailed upon it like ships in line, leaving a trail of widening 'V's' behind them. Scores of chickens pecked in the dirt nearby.

It is a scene so familiar we barely notice it. There is nothing remarkable about this farm; there is no secret garden, there are no talking animals making cunning plans. It is observed from the outside, and if it seems a bit clichéd, we barely pay attention.

Jane begs Adam to tell her how he performs his magic, and he is unable to do so. And she believes he is being cruel, for every man she has known has been cruel to her. Her father and her brother have convinced her that she is clumsy, ugly, stupid, that she does not belong with them. She is repeatedly locked alone in her room, deemed unfit for human society. And she assumes Adam is the same.

But he relents. He says that the magic that flows in him is the same magic that flows in the farm. No magician's trick, he says, can ever explain how a chicken produces an egg, how an oak grows from an acorn, how clouds shift form. This world, he insists, is the greatest magic there is. It is the same magic Mary and Colin find in the garden, the magic of things as they are.

Adam also gives Jane what he calls 'Me' magic, telling her that if she can hold on to memories of her happiest times, they will not only console her when she is sad, but they will give her great strength, the ability to know herself and move forwards.

A cynical reader might dismiss these passages. But for my mother, I believe, they were transformative. I cannot tell you that she fell in love with my father because he was like Adam; I cannot tell you that she wanted a little farm because she remembered the farm in this book. But I am pretty confident that this is what happened. For my mother learned who she was through stories, and she changed who she was because of stories.

In later years, her favourite film was Lars von Trier's *Breaking the Waves*. It is, initially, harder to imagine a work more unlike Gallico's novel, although certainly part of the appeal for my mother was a briefly glimpsed extra, one of the oil workers, who looks extraordinarily like my father did in the 1970s. But the story she saw was the same. A young woman is alone, completely alone, in a house, a community, that rejects everything about her. And a stranger comes, and she falls completely in love. And she loses him. And there is, in the end, some form of salvation. All stories became, for her, stories of salvation.

The salvation at the end of *The Man Who Was Magic* is far simpler than that of *Breaking the Waves*. Jane walks to the farm, now in autumn, and remembers it in the summer: 'It had all been strong enchantment once. Why could it not be again?' And she remembers, at length, every incident from her earlier picnic. She remembers that she once was loved. And the memory is sufficient, and she goes on her way, rejoicing.

I cannot tell you that *The Man Who Was Magic* is a perfect book. It has, at times, a veneer of racism that might be common to its time but is deeply unappealing now, and that I sorely wish was not there. And like so many of the books I've mentioned, it is deeply patriarchal. Looking at my childhood reading, I am astonished to find how uniform the authors are, not just that I read so many men, but that I read so many white men born in the final years of the nineteenth century. The books that shaped me emerged from a particular world that neither my mother nor I would want to claim any part of; it is an uncomfortable inheritance. These stories, which champion the marginalised and the dispossessed, have been written by those in power; rather than seeking to challenge the construction of the world, they simply expand it on the same principles. And yes, it is a sentimental story, wilfully unsophisticated.

And yet.

You may not know this book, just as you may not know my mother, but I hope you have a book like it, a loved one like her. Because the moral of every book here, in a sense, is that it is alright to love the ordinary. These books teach us to love the fields and forests and all who live within them. They teach us that what we first encounter in childhood remains with us always. And this is a lesson that we, that I, still need. We do not have to love the extraordinary only; we can love what we already know. My mother, to me, was extraordinary, and yet her life, in some sense, was as ordinary as can be imagined.

My mother does not have a headstone, as I write, sixteen years after her death. We buried her ashes on a rainy Sunday morning, and although we were in the Catholic cemetery, and you would imagine that there were people who would do this sort of thing, we dug the grave ourselves, my father and I, two broken men standing in the mud. The man at the crematorium was from Glasgow, it turned out, and he knew I had to return to Scotland the next day, and so he'd moved my mother's incineration to the front of the queue, and had returned her cremains, that most horrible word, to us still warm. I pressed her bones against my cheek, as if it was her last breath. And then we buried them.

I have not been back to that cemetery in a decade. I read about it just a month after the funeral, in the *London Review of Books*, for on the very same day we buried my mother, in the Jewish portion of the cemetery across the street, Saul Bellow was buried, surrounded by the great literary figures of the time. If I had looked up I would have seen James Wood, Martin Amis, the men whose work filled my teenage years. But I did not need them. And yet I needed a memorial. And so I had a wooden block engraved to sit on the shelf at the Glasgow Women's Library, reading simply 'For my mother who, like Julian of Norwich, sought in solitude for the love that sustains everything.'

My mother's solitude and my own are very different. But in the books we read, the lives we lived outside ourselves, I believe we may have found that love.

Today, reading another text entirely, a work of mourning by the poet Ocean Vuong, I'm reminded of Roland Barthes's *Mourning Diary*, kept in the years following his mother's death. Near the start Barthes begins an entry with an ellipsis: '...that this death fails to destroy me altogether means that I want to live wildly, madly, and that therefore the fear of my own death is always there, not displaced by a single inch.' I do not know if I have ever lived wildly or madly, but the fear is there, always. There is no day, scarcely an hour, when I am not aware of my death, when it does not haunt me. I want to live the life my mother wanted for me; I want my survival to mean something.

A year and a half later Barthes writes, on the very day I was born, about 'everything that in my heart keeps me from loving myself.' And this rings more true. I cannot mend what I have lost. I cannot wholly forgive myself. And I am uncomfortable, now, quoting these words of Barthes that he never intended anyone to read, uncomfortable mining Vuong's story for the moments that resonate with my own life. But I cannot do otherwise.

To write your mother, says Vuong, is to change her body: 'by writing, I mar it. I change, embellish, and preserve you all at once.' To write your mother is to transfigure her, and that preservation entails loss. Every gap in her life that I fill takes something away from her.

And yet, I persist. Writing these words, reading these books, is the closest I can come to a way back. I do not know if it is enough, and yet it must be sufficient. It must be everything. Because I do not want you just to understand my mother; I want you to love her. I want to make her alive again through these stories. I want you to tell them to yourself, to see her life in relation to your own.

So one last story, a short one, not a children's story at all. A figure sits on a bus. I imagine her as a young woman, but it could be me, or you, or anyone at all. The bus winds through country roads, past small villages and fields. The bus is boarded by strangers, who speak among themselves, names and stories that you do not know, but which are somehow still familiar. The passengers speak of the immanent and the eternal. And the bus judders to a stop. There is a moose in the road, huge, unknowable, intimate. And the passengers stare, and then they begin to move again, on their way into the night.

'Why, why do we feel / (we all feel) this sweet / sensation of joy?', writes Elizabeth Bishop, for this is her story, her poem 'The Moose' that I am telling you. And she knows the answer. We all do. It is the joy of encounter, the joy of community, the joy of loving that which surprises us. It is the joy of seeing our lives as a path, and seeing it broken. It is the joy of devoting yourself, for just a moment, to a relationship that cannot be sustained.

We all feel it.

I did not read Bishop until I was in college, and I heard her more than I read her, for we went to the same college, Bishop and I, and every visiting poet would open their reading with one of her poems. Bishop became a common language, a shared experience. And reading *Geography III* in full for the first time several years later, sitting in the afternoon sun on a lunchbreak, I suddenly saw my mother there too, saw her sitting in the waiting room reading *National Geographic* magazine, saw her walking on the beach, saw her losing everything. Every story that I read becomes the story of my mother.

For weeks, months after my mother died I had trouble walking down city streets. The first few days I would look into strangers' faces and ask myself 'how do they not know? The world has ended, and how do they not know?' And then it changed, and I became filled with empathy, so that I would see in those faces all the tragedies that I did not know. If reading these books has taught me anything, it is that all of my stories are individual, and all of them are universal. What we share is the unshareability of our grief.

But we share our joy, too. We share the joy of knowing that we have loved, and that love has made us more than ourselves. And we share those other worlds we inhabit, the worlds of books and creatures, the worlds that make us more than what we are.

We are alone, you and I. However hard we try, we do not know how to make sense of our loss. We cannot bring the dead to life; we cannot make them real. But we can see them in our communities, in their presence and their absence. We can see them sharing that life that goes around and through us, of which we all have only the tiniest part. We can see their joy. We can see them in our stories. We can read them back.

What do people who feel this bad do? I still don't know. But I try to tell the truth, and when I can't, I tell stories. Try to make it rain butterflies, just for a moment.

Notes

The Story of Babar

p. 5 Jean de Brunhoff. *The Story of Babar, The Little Elephant* (London: Egmont, 2008), 34.

Merle the High Flying Squirrel

p. 11 Bill Peet. *Merle the High Flying Squirrel* (Boston, MA: Houghton Mifflin, 1974), 1.

p. 12 Peet, *Merle the High Flying Squirrel*, 2.

p. 12 Gail F. Melson. *Why the Wild Things Are: Animals in the Lives of Children* (Cambridge, MA and London: Harvard University Press, 2001), 150.

p. 12 Tess Cosslett. *Talking Animals in British Children's Fiction, 1786–1914* (Farnham: Ashgate, 2006), 73.

p. 14 Michelle Superle. 'Animal Heroes and Transforming Substances: Canine Characters in Contemporary Children's Literature'. In *Animals and the Human Imagination: A Companion to Animal* Studies, ed. Aaron Gross and Anne Vallely (New York: Columbia University Press, 2012), 174.

p. 14 Nicole E. Larsen, Kang Lee, and Patricia A. Ganea. 'Do Storybooks with Anthropomorphized Animal Characters Promote Prosocial Behaviors in Young Children?' *Developmental Science* 21 (2018): e12590. doi: 10.1111/desc.12590.

p. 15 Else Holmelund Minarik. *Little Bear's Friend* (New York: HarperCollins, 1960).

p. 16 Arnold Lobel. *Mouse Tales* (New York: HarperCollins, 1972).

p. 16 Arnold Lobel. *Frog and Toad Tales* (Tadsworth: World's Work, 1976), 115.

p. 17 Maurice Sendak. *Where the Wild Things Are* (New York: Harper Trophy, 1984), n.p.

p. 18 Gaston Bachelard. *The Poetics of Space*, trans. Maria Jolas (Boston, MA: Beacon Press, 1994), 3.

p. 21 John Waters. 'Ladies and Gentleman... The Nicest Kids in Town! Keeping the Memory of The Buddy Deane Show Alive'. *Baltimore* (April 1985). www. baltimoremagazine.com/1985/4/1/john-waters-on-keeping-the-memory-of-the-buddy-deane-show-alive.

p. 21 Laura Wexler. 'The Messy Truth of The Real "Hairspray"'. *The Washington Post*, 17 September 2003. www.washingtonpost.com/archive/lifestyle/2003/09/17/the-messy-truth-of-the-real-hairspray.

p. 24 L. Frank Baum. *Oz: The Complete Collection, Volume I: The Wonderful Wizard of Oz, The Marvelous Land of Oz, Ozma of Oz* (London: Simon & Schuster, 2013), 406.

p. 24 Baum, *Oz: The Complete Collection*, 438.

p. 24 Baum, *Oz: The Complete Collection*, 470.

p. 25 Baum, *Oz: The Complete Collection*, 573.

Charlotte's Web

p. 31 Randall Jarrell. *The Animal Family* (New York: HarperCollins, 1993), 179–80.

p. 33 Robert Urquhart. *Ordinary Choices: Individuals, Incommensurability, and Democracy* (London and New York: Routledge, 2005), 2.

p. 33 Stephen Sondheim. *Look, I Made a Hat: Collected Lyrics (1981–2011), with Attendant Comments, Amplifications, Dogmas, Harangues, Digressions, Anecdotes and Miscellany* (London: Virgin, 2011), 52.

p. 35 E. B. White. *Charlotte's Web* (London: Puffin, 2014), 1.

p. 35 Amy Ratelle. *Animality and Children's Literature and Film* (Basingstoke: Palgrave Macmillan, 2015), 10.

p. 36 White, *Charlotte's Web*, 108.

p. 37 Walter R. Brooks. *Freddy the Detective* (New York: Puffin, 2001).

p. 37 White, *Charlotte's Web*, 85.

p. 38 White, *Charlotte's Web*, 197.

p. 38 White, *Charlotte's Web*, 222.

p. 39 White, *Charlotte's Web*, 232.

p. 39 White, *Charlotte's Web*, 249.

p. 40 White, *Charlotte's Web*, 84–85.

The Wind in the Willows

p. 41 Alison Bechdel. *Fun Home: A Family Tragicomic* (London: Jonathan Cape, 2006), 146–47.

p. 42 Lynda Barry. *One! Hundred! Demons!* (Seattle, WA: Sasquatch Books, 2002), 212.

p. 42 Lucy Mangan. *Bookworm: A Memoir of Childhood Reading* (London: Vintage, 2018), 177.

p. 42 Peter Hunt. *The Making of The Wind in the Willows* (Oxford: Bodleian Library, 2018), 88.

p. 42 Kenneth Grahame. *The Wind in the Willows* (London: Methuen, 1969), 269.

p. 42 Grahame, *The Wind in the Willows*, 257.

p. 44 Wendy Lesser. *Nothing Remains the Same: Rereading and Remembering* (Boston, MA and New York: Houghton Mifflin, 2002), 4.

p. 45 Patricia Meyer Spacks. *On Rereading* (Cambridge, MA and London: Belknap/Harvard University Press, 2011).

p. 45 Matei Călinescu. *Rereading* (New Haven, CT and London: Yale University Press, 1993), xi.

p. 46 Grahame, *The Wind in the Willows*, 10.

p. 46 Grahame, *The Wind in the Willows*, 99.

p. 46 Grahame, *The Wind in the Willows*, 102.

p. 47 James Wood. *The Nearest Thing to Life* (London: Jonathan Cape, 2015), 114.

p. 50 Elspeth Grahame. 'Introduction'. In *First Whisper of The Wind in the Willows*, by Kenneth Grahame, ed. Elspeth Grahame (London: Methuen, 1944), 27.

p. 50 Matthew Dennison. *Eternal Boy: The Life of Kenneth Grahame* (London: Head of Zeus, 2018), 243.

p. 51 Grahame, *The Wind in the Willows*, 54–55.

p. 52 Dionne Brand. *An Autobiography of the Autobiography of Reading* (Edmonton, AB: University of Alberta Press, 2020), 8.

p. 54 Rudyard Kipling. *Something of Myself and Other Autobiographical Writings*, ed. Thomas Pinney (Cambridge: Cambridge University Press, 1990), 70.

p. 54 C. S. Lewis. *Selected Literary Essays*, ed. Walter Hooper (Cambridge: Cambridge University Press, 1969), 232.

p. 55 Rudyard Kipling. *The Jungle Books*, ed. Daniel Karlin (London: Penguin Classics, 2000), 298.

p. 55 Ernest Thompson Seton. *Wild Animals I Have Known* (Toronto, ON: McClelland and Stewart, 1977), 11.

p. 55 Ralph H. Lutts. *The Nature Fakers: Wildlife, Science and Sentiment* (Golden, CO: Fulcrum, 1990), 151.

The Magician's Nephew

p. 64. Derek Jarman. *Modern Nature: The Journals of Derek Jarman* (London: Vintage, 2018), 81.

p. 65 Sharmila Sarkar, Sudip Kumar Ghosh, Debabrata Bandyopadhyay, and Saswati Nath. 'Psychogenic Purpura'. *Indian Journal of Psychiatry* 55(2) (2013): 192–94. doi: 10.4103/0019-5545.111463.

p. 66 Mohammad Jafferany and Gaurav Bhattacharya. 'Psychogenic Purpura (Gardner-Diamond Syndrome)'. *The Primary Care Companion for CNS Disorders* 17(1) (2015). doi: 10.4088/PCC.14br01697.

p. 68 Francis Spufford. *The Child that Books Built: A Memoir of Childhood and Reading* (London: Faber, 2002), 101.

p. 69 Alison Waller. *Rereading Childhood Books: A Poetics* (London: Bloomsbury Academic, 2019), 144.

p. 69 Anne Fadiman. 'Foreword: On Rereading'. In *Rereadings: Seventeen Writers Revisit Books They Love*, ed. Fadiman (New York: Farrar, Straus, and Giroux, 2005), xxi.

p. 70 C. S. Lewis. *The Magician's Nephew* (London: Bodley Head, 1971), 28.

p. 72 Lewis, *The Magician's Nephew*, 140.

p. 72 Lewis, *The Magician's Nephew*, 173.

p. 73 Spufford, *The Child that Books Built*, 99.

p. 73 C. S. Lewis. *A Grief Observed* (New York: HarperOne, 1994), 54.

p. 74 George MacDonald. *The Princess and Curdie* (London: Jane Nissen, 2013).

p. 75 Fahad Aziz and Dana F. Clark. 'Introduction to Kidney Transplantation'. In *Kidney Transplant Management: A Guide to Evaluation and Comorbidities*, ed. Sandesh Parajuli and Fahad Aziz (Cham: Springer, 2019), 1–3.

p. 75 William E. Braun. 'Long-term Complications of Renal Transplantation'. *Kidney International* 37 (1990): 1363–78.

p. 76 Jean-Luc Nancy. *Corpus*, trans. Richard A. Rand (Stanford, CA: Stanford University Press), 163.

Watership Down

p. 78 Patrick J. Kiger. 'The Cult Next Door'. *Baltimore* (February 1994): 34–55. www.scribd.com/doc/76725336/Lamb-of-God-a-Branch-of-the-SOS-And-Its-Troubles.

p. 79 Kiger, 'The Cult Next Door', 36.

p. 81 Judith Church Tydings. 'Shipwrecked in the Spirit: Implications of Some Controversial Catholic Movements'. *Cultic Studies Journal* 16(2) (1999): 83–179.

p. 82 Richard Adams. *Watership Down* (London: Puffin, 1973), 15.

p. 83 Adams, *Watership Down*, 169.

p. 84 Adams, *Watership Down*, 180.

p. 85 Kiger, 'The Cult Next Door', 53.

p. 86 Kiger, 'The Cult Next Door', 55.

p. 86 Adams, *Watership Down*, 459.

p. 87 Adams, *Watership Down*, 463.

p. 87 R. W. Lockley. *The Private Life of the Rabbit* (London: Andre Deutsch, 1964), 144.

p. 88 Adams, *Watership Down*, 478.

p. 89 John Humphrey Noyes. *History of American Socialisms* (New York: Dover, 1966), 351–53.

p. 90 Benjamin Zablocki. *Alienation and Charisma: A Study of Contemporary American Communes* (New York: Free Press, 1980), 185.

p. 91 Zablocki, *Alienation and Charisma*, 323.

p. 91 Noyes, *History of American Socialisms*, 588–89.

p. 94 Spencer Klaw. *Without Sin: The Life and Death of the Oneida Community* (New York: Penguin, 1993).

p. 94 Kiger, 'The Cult Next Door', 36.

p. 95 Pierrepont Noyes. *My Father's House: An Oneida Boyhood* (New York: Holt, Rinehart and Winston, 1965), 3.

p. 95 Noyes, *My Father's House*, 18.

p. 95 Paul Kagan. *New World Utopias: A Photographic History of the Search for Community* (New York: Penguin, 1975), 179–81.

p. 96 Julian of Norwich. *Revelations of Divine Love*, trans. Barry Windeatt (Oxford: World's Classics, 2015), 4–5.

p. 98 Marilynne Robinson. *When I Was a Child I Read Books* (London: Virago, 2012), 20–21.

The Secret Garden

p. 101 Meera Atkinson. *The Poetics of Transgenerational Trauma* (London: Bloomsbury, 2017), 61.

p. 103 Judith Herman. *Trauma and Recovery* (New York: Basic Books, 1997), 51.

p. 103 Nicholas Abraham and Maria Torok. *The Shell and the Kernel*, vol. 1, ed. and trans. Nicholas T. Rand (Chicago, IL and London: University of Chicago Press), 171.

p. 105 Virginia Woolf. *Moments of Being: Autobiographical Writings*, ed. Jeanne Schulkind, new edn (London: Pimlico, 2002), 11.

p. 106 Alison Bechdel. *Are You My Mother?: A Comic Drama* (London: Jonathan Cape, 2012), 288–89.

p. 107 Katherine Angel. *Daddy Issues* (London: Peninsula Press, 2019), 105.

p. 108 Jacqueline Rose. *Mothers: An Essay on Love and Cruelty* (London: Faber, 2018), 37.

p. 108 Frances Hodgson Burnett. *The Secret Garden* (Harmondsworth: Puffin, 1994), 1.

p. 109 D. W. Winnicott. *Home is Where We Start From: Essays by a Psychoanalyst*, ed. Clare Winnicott, Ray Shepherd, and Madeleine Davis (London: Penguin, 1990), 22.

p. 109 D. W. Winnicott. *The Child, the Family and the Outside World* (London: Penguin, 1991), 228.

p. 110 Burnett, *The Secret Garden*, 25.

p. 111 Burnett, *The Secret Garden*, 89.

p. 112 Burnett, *The Secret Garden*, 186.

p. 113 Burnett, *The Secret Garden*, 237.

p. 113 Burnett, *The Secret Garden*, 216.

p. 114 Jakob von Uexküll. *A Foray into the Worlds of Animals and Humans* with *A Theory of Meaning*, trans. Joseph D. O'Neil (Minneapolis, MN and London: University of Minnesota Press, 2010).

p. 116 Annie Dillard. *Holy the Firm* (New York: Harper & Row, 1977), 76.

p. 116 Virginia Woolf. *The Death of a Moth and Other Essays* (London: Hogarth, 1947), 9–10.

The Book of the Dun Cow

p. 117 Robert Kiely. 'A Fable for Our Time'. *The New York Times*, 10 December 1978. www.nytimes.com/1978/12/10/archives/a-fable-for-our-time-fable.html.

p. 118 Walter Wangerin, Jr. *The Book of the Dun Cow* (London: Hodder and Stoughton, 1990), 5.

p. 119 Wangerin, *The Book of the Dun Cow*, 89.

p. 119 Wangerin, *The Book of the Dun Cow*, 226.

p. 120 Melanie Klein. *Love, Guilt and Reparation and Other Works 1921–1945* (London: Vintage, 1998), 343.

p. 123 Walter Wangerin, Jr. *The Book of Sorrows* (San Francisco, CA: Harper & Row, 1985), 225.

p. 127 Klein, *Love, Guilt and Reparation*, 362.

p. 127 Valerie Krips. *The Presence of the Past: Memory, Heritage, and Childhood in Postwar Britain* (London and New York: Routledge, 2000), 15.

p. 127 Margaret Mackey. *One Child Reading: My Auto-Bibliography* (Edmonton, AB: University of Alberta Press, 2016), 507.

p. 129 D. W. Winnicott. 'Reparation in Respect of Mother's Organized Defence against Depression'. In *Collected Papers: Through Paediatrics to Psych-Analysis* (New York: Basic Books, 1958), 91–96.

p. 130 Simone de Beauvoir. *A Very Easy Death*, trans. Patrick O'Brian (New York: Pantheon, 1999), 94.

The Man Who Was Magic

p. 131 Leila Aboulela. *Elsewhere, Home* (London: Telegram, 2018), 53.

p. 132 Paul Gallico. *Jennie* (Harmondsworth: Penguin, 1963), 63.

p. 133 Gallico, *Jennie*, 147–48.

p. 133 Carl Safina. *Beyond Words: What Animals Think and Feel* (New York: Henry Holt, 2015), 29.

p. 134 Vinciane Despret. *What Would Animals Say If We Asked the Right Questions?*, trans. Brett Buchanan (Minneapolis, MN and London: University of Minnesota Press, 2016), 173.

p. 134 Jenny Diski. *What I Don't Know about Animals* (London: Virago, 2010), 284.

p. 135 A. L. Kennedy. *On Writing* (London: Jonathan Cape, 2013), 275.

p. 136 Gallico, *Jennie*, 233.

p. 136 Gallico, *Jennie*, 234.

p. 138 Paul Gallico. *The Man Who Was Magic* (New York: Doubleday, 1966), 181.

p. 140 Gallico, *The Man Who Was Magic*, 102.

p. 141 Gallico, *The Man Who Was Magic*, 200.

p. 144 Roland Barthes. *Mourning Diary*, trans. Richard Howard (New York: Hill and Wang, 2010), 21.

p. 144 Barthes, *Mourning Diary*, 219.

p. 144 Ocean Vuong. *On Earth We're Briefly Gorgeous* (London: Jonathan Cape, 2019), 85.

p. 145 Elizabeth Bishop. *Geography III* (New York: Farrar, Straus and Giroux, 1984), 30.

Acknowledgements

This book could never have been written without the support, encouragement, and detailed comments of Peggy Hughes, Elizabeth Anderson, Noémi Keresztes, and Caitlin Beveridge, each of whom, in their own ways, changed everything. I'm also eternally grateful to other early readers, especially Shona Potts, Helen Lynch, and Julia Kotzur.

For advice and support, at different stages, I am also indebted to my friends and colleagues at the University of Aberdeen, as well as to everyone at Goldsmiths, especially Susan Kelly, and to the book's peer reviewers. I am grateful to some of those who have heard these stories over the years, and asked for more: Emma-Lee Davidson, Leslie Drury, Robert Eaglestone, Polly Grice, Katherine Furman, Jessica Golub Law, Abigail Miller, Jess Mullen, Laurie Jones Neighbors, Noel Reddy, and Linda Tym. There are too many names to list here, of everyone who has offered support along the way, but you are all in my heart.

My greatest debt is to my father, David Baker, who answered my questions when I asked them and didn't ask any of his own. This is not the version of the story he would tell, but he has made it all possible.